Prai:

On Earth
AS IT IS IN
Heaven

RESTORING GOD'S VISION OF
RACE AND DISCIPLESHIP

In *On Earth as It Is in Heaven*, Fr. Josh Johnson offers his readers insight into how racism has affected the Catholic Church in the United States, as well as how Catholics everywhere can join the effort to eradicate the sin of racism in our Church. His personal anecdotes, inspiring life histories of holy African-American Catholics, and concrete suggestions for individual and common action will aid Catholics to work together for racial reconciliation, healing, and renewal in the Church.

—Wilton Cardinal Gregory,
Archbishop of Washington, DC

On Earth as It Is in Heaven is a compelling rallying cry for racial justice and healing from a promising young voice of the New Evangelization. Drawing on the wisdom of Scripture, the pain of personal experience, and the words and witness of figures such as Venerable Augustus Tolton, Pope St. John Paul II, and Martin Luther King, Fr. Josh Johnson reminds us of our mission to draw "all tribes and peoples" (Revelation 7:9) into the body of Christ. He challenges us to confront our nation's original sin of slavery, and to work to combat racism in our parish communities, not just with words but with intentional action. Yet he emphasizes that this difficult work—like all of the Church's social justice efforts— requires that we stay centered on Christ and his Real Presence in the Blessed Sacrament. This book will be a great help to many Catholics in the pews wanting to take a first but important step in this direction. I warmly recommend it.

—Bishop Robert Barron, Auxiliary Bishop of Los Angeles
and founder of Word on Fire

Considering the themes of spiritual renewal, evangelization, and personal conversion for this new millennium, Father Johnson makes a compelling case for the connections between race and Christian discipleship. He offers recommendations for bringing the gospel to hardened and not so hardened hearts grounded from personal experiences of his youth and as a pastor, and elucidated by factual public events, both positive and negative, that report on the societal struggle with neighborly regard. I recommend his book as a rich contribution for private spiritual reading, adult religious education, book clubs, and group discussion on how the Church can be a genuine beacon of racial reconciliation.

—Most Reverend Joseph N. Perry,
Auxiliary Bishop, Archdiocese of Chicago

Fr. Josh Johnson is a gift to the Church. His transparency in ministry affirms many to live out lives of holiness. His witness also challenges those in the Church to turn away from America's "original sin" of racism and see each other as brothers and sisters made in God's image. This book takes the reader on this journey of pain, love, and hope.

—Dr. Ansel Augustine, Catholic speaker and author

On Earth as It Is in Heaven is a much-needed book about race and discipleship in the Catholic Church. Father Josh casts a truth-filled vision of hope for the Church drawing from spiritual practices, historical context, and his own personal narrative. A timely resource that is an ideal blend of prophetic, pastoral, and practical wisdom for a divided Church in need of healing. Yet, it goes much deeper than that. It is a book about deep abiding communion with the Trinity and the heart of heaven for every tribe and tongue to dwell in unity. This book is a John 17 invitation from the Holy Spirit to join in on the restorative Spirit work of the kingdom to make us all one (John 17:21).

—Michelle Benzinger, cohost of the Abiding Together
Podcast, creative director, and speaker

Many American Catholics want to have conversations about the persistence of racial injustice in our country and in our Church, but don't know how to. Fr. Josh Johnson's *On Earth as It Is in Heaven* is a readable, inviting, and theologically rich entry point to this pressing discussion, one which should involve Catholics of every tribe and tongue. I can't recommend this challenging, spiritually enriching, and extremely informative book enough. It is an important and accessible launching point for a high-school and up readership—perfect material for parish discussion groups and those in ministry and education.

—Dr. Shaun Blanchard, Catholic theologian and senior research fellow, National Institute for Newman Studies

The Program for Priestly Formation calls for the candidate for priesthood to be a bridge to the community. In his ministry, Fr. Josh Johnson serves as an excellent example of this quality of priestly leadership, and his book *On Earth as It Is in Heaven* summons us to reflect on how to practice this ideal. Fr. Johnson's personal experience and spiritual journey qualifies him to speak so authoritatively on this topic. This is a must read for all who seek to bridge the racial divide that challenges those who seek leadership in the church.

—Fr. Gregory M. Boquet, president-rector, Saint Joseph Seminary College

Drawing from Sacred Scripture, Church tradition, history, the witness of courageous women and men, and personal experiences, Fr. Josh proves to be a powerful voice for Catholics and anyone who desires to be part of the solution to address the racial divisions in our country and our Church. This book provides a path forward, not only for us to heal our land of this sin but also to become the authentic and intentional disciples that Jesus Christ has called us to be.

—Fr. Robert Boxie, priest chaplain, Howard University, Washington, DC

Fr. Josh Johnson speaks with love, conviction, and urgency when he calls on Catholics to "accompany people of all races, ethnicities, and languages in discipleship." Jesus gave permission to the world to judge whether we are authentic when He said, "By this all men will know that you are my disciples, if you have love for one another." Not only do *"I"* need to be transformed by the power of the Eucharist, but *"we"* need to be transformed together as witnesses to the world. If we want to see the world change, *On Earth as It Is in Heaven* gives us the tools to begin this work!

—*Jeff Cavins, author, podcaster, pilgrimage guide, and creator of* The Great Adventure *Bible Study Program*

Powerful! *On Earth as It Is in Heaven* invites readers to curiosity and courage as they strive to better understand racial relations within the United States and the American Catholic Church. Rooted in Scripture and accompanied by prayerful practices, Father Josh Johnson journeys with us on a mind, heart, and soul level. It is evident that his own prayer life and relationship with Jesus Christ add generously to the depths of this incredibly timely and meaningful book.

—*Sister Desiré Anne-Marie Findlay, vocation director,* Congregation of the Sisters of St. Felix

As the first Black priest in the Diocese of Lexington, I want to invite you to use this book as a devotional for your relationship with God and as a resource in your fight against racial injustices. *On Earth as It Is in Heaven* provides insights rooted in both the Sacred Scriptures and in the lives of the Black Catholics on the road to sainthood that can help the reader to identify, address, and rise above the sins of racism. It is my hope that you will be inspired by Fr. Johnson's reflections to build God's kingdom by cultivating unity and racial healing in our beautifully diverse human family.

—*Fr. Norman Fischer Jr., vice president,* The National Black Catholic Clergy Caucus

On Earth as It Is in Heaven lives up to its title. In this book, Father Joshua, with the gift of his own straightforward yet profound style, shows us how the ordinary work of building relationships, facing fears, and taking on the challenges of racism that manifest in our daily lives here on earth, can help us to, as individuals and as a Church, enter into the heavenly and eternal mind, heart, and desires of Christ; that we may be one in him.

—*Sister Josephine Garrett,* Sisters of the Holy Family of Nazareth, *nationally certified and licensed counselor*

This book is a synthetic moment in the life of the Church. Fr. Josh keeps his focus on the Eucharist, the sacraments, heaven, and evangelization. From that center, he shows how racism in history, policy, or practice is sinful precisely because it contradicts both our identity as disciples and the biblical vision of heaven. In a particular way this book will appeal to seminarians because Fr. Josh provides a blueprint for how to engage questions of race in a way that proceeds from and returns to the heart of the Catholic Faith.

—*Dr. Ed Hogan, academic dean,* Kenrick-Glennon Seminary

With great faith, prophetic honesty, and a bold commitment to the fullness of truth in the Gospel, Fr. Josh Johnson's new book *On Earth as It Is in Heaven* calls us to reflect on the gift of unity proposed by the kingdom of heaven, how the horrific sin of racism has wounded (and hindered) the mission and effectiveness of the Church, and how we can be vessels of God's work of reconciling all things to himself.

—*Matt Maher, Catholic singer and songwriter*

In *On Earth as It Is in Heaven*, Fr. Josh Johnson has given the Church a tremendous gift. This is a beautiful, powerful, challenging book. Every Catholic in the United States (and beyond) should read it. And not just read it. Study it, pray about it, discuss it, and then ask God to help us work together to make the Church on earth a living mirror of the Church in heaven, in which people from "every nation, race, people, and tongue" are truly one in the body of Christ (Revelation 7:9, NAB).

—Dr. Brant Pitre, author of Jesus and the Jewish Roots of the Eucharist

Father Joshua takes us on a journey toward holiness by sharing stories of saints, everyday people, and even of himself. The practical steps he outlines in this book are doable if you have the heart for greater conversion. He opens our eyes to matters that perhaps we have never considered, and he does this gently and with encouragement to repentance and conversion. This book should be read in every seminary and diocese in the United States.

—Gloria Purvis, Catholic speaker, podcaster, and radio host

Fr. Joshua Johnson has captured the spirit of the struggles that many People of Color face in the Catholic Church. The stories that he shares will certainly resonate with Black men and women who've had similar experiences in seminary formation, religious life, and parish ministries. *On Earth as It Is in Heaven* takes the reader on an engaging journey that will assure them that they are not alone. Fr. Johnson's personal reflections and meditations on the lives of the clergy, religious, and laity who have gone before us, give hope for all of us to persevere in our call to missionary discipleship and sacrificial service in our journey with God.

—Very Rev. Michael L. Thompson, SSJ, Josephite Superior General Emeritus

Our purpose on earth is to mirror heaven. Providing the rich and far-reaching history of the African Catholic Church, Fr. Josh shows that the early Christians found fertile soil in Africa. Proof of this is given through the notable African popes and the many Black saints. While the Catholic Church in Africa continues to grow, the Church in America is not experiencing similar supernatural fruit with people of color in our land. Not only does *On Earth as It Is in Heaven* present readers with Fr. Josh's reasoning for the racial divide in American Catholicism, but it also provides tools that can help all people "join together at the Eucharistic table."

**—*Valerie E. Washington, executive director,*
The National Black Catholic Congress**

I appreciate how Father Johnson reflects on his own lived experience while also drawing from the spiritual, theological, and liturgical tradition of the Church to address a fundamental obstacle for true communion in the Church—racial inequality. The reflections that Father Johnson provides are quite important for seminarians, clergy and laity, those preparing for ministry in the Church, and for those who coordinate ministry. Evangelization cannot authentically occur if the matter of race is not properly addressed. Father Johnson provides us with sound challenges for anyone who claims to be a disciple of Jesus!

**—*Very Reverend James A. Wehner, STD,*
has served as rector of Notre Dame Seminary, New Orleans,
the Pontifical College Josephinum, Ohio,
*and Saint Paul Seminary, Pittsburgh.***

✝ ✝ ✝

FR. JOSH JOHNSON

On Earth

AS IT IS IN
Heaven

**RESTORING GOD'S VISION OF
RACE AND DISCIPLESHIP**

ASCENSION

West Chester, Pennsylvania

Excerpts from the English translation of the *Catechism of the Catholic Church* for use in the United States of America © 1994 United States Catholic Conference, Inc.-Libreria Editrice Vaticana. Used with permission. English translation of the *Catechism of the Catholic Church: Modifications from the Editio Typica* © 1997 United States Conference of Catholic Bishops–Libreria Editrice Vaticana.

Unless otherwise noted, Scripture passages are from the Revised Standard Version Bible–Second Catholic Edition © 2006 by the Division of Christian Education of the National Council of the Churches of Christ in the United States of America. Used by permission. All rights reserved.

Ascension
PO Box 1990
West Chester, PA 19380
1-800-376-0520
ascensionpress.com

Cover design: Rosemary Strohm

Printed in the United States of America
22 23 24 25 26 5 4 3 2 1
ISBN 978-1-950784-80-6

CONTENTS

An Invitation from Fr. Josh

"For with God nothing will be impossible."

− Luke 1:37

Venerable Fr. Augustus Tolton (1854–1897) was born into slavery and eventually became a priest. In the Scriptures, Jesus promises his disciples that we will suffer persecution, and Fr. Tolton certainly underwent many unimaginable hardships throughout his life and ministry as a priest.

Fr. Tolton and I have many things in common. He was the first recognized African American priest in the United States—and, for a time, was the *only* one. Currently, I am the only African American priest ordained to serve in the Diocese of Baton Rouge. Fr. Tolton's vocation was nurtured through his consistent time that he set apart on his schedule to be in the presence of the Eucharist. Likewise, I spent many hours in Eucharistic Adoration discerning whether God was calling me to enter the seminary, and I have continued to spend at least an hour a day with Jesus in Blessed Sacrament throughout my priesthood. As a priest, Fr. Tolton tirelessly emptied himself out in the service of people from every racial, ethnic, and socio-economic background—and I have tried to emulate his example in my priestly ministry as well.

Though he and I share many similarities in our vocations, our lives are also marked by stark differences. When Fr. Tolton was ordained in 1886, he ministered to nineteenth-century Catholics in America, many of whom were hostile toward him for no other reason than the color of his skin. He was ignored by many Catholic lay people, rejected by many of his brother priests, and discriminated against by the laws that were established in his lifetime. At that time, Black people were not legally afforded the same opportunities as their white brothers and sisters in Christ. I cannot imagine how difficult it was for him to persevere in his vocation as a priest with so little support from the Church.

Fast forward to my ordination in 2014. By the grace of God, I am happy to affirm that things are so different! In my priesthood, I have been welcomed by the majority of the Catholic laity, accepted by most of my brothers in the priesthood, and am legally afforded the same opportunities as every other American citizen. It is important for all of us to pause for a moment and collectively praise God for how much progress we have made, both in our nation and as a Church, regarding race relations.

We have come a long way in healing the racial wounds of many centuries and in transforming the many racially unjust systems that divided America for so long. Slavery and legalized segregation are a thing of the past. Young people have role models in people of color who are leaders in our Church, in business, and in government. We now have African Americans serving as bishops in the Church, coaches and managers in professional sports, and CEOs of major corporations. Black people have been elected senators and representatives, state legislators, governors, and even president of the United States.

These are great strides, and we need to keep this progress in mind. Nonetheless, these very significant advances should not cause us to settle for the status quo. There is always more work to be done on this side of heaven. Today, nearly sixty years removed from the era of legalized segregation and discrimination, we continue to see evidence of ongoing racial division, both in America and in our Church. This division certainly does not console the heart of Jesus, who prayed that we may all be one (see John 17).

As disciples of Jesus Christ in the twenty-first century, we still have work to do in bringing about the unity to which he calls us. As our Lord tells us, nothing is impossible for God (see Luke 1:37). We have been called by our Lord to be the saints of this generation, to pray and work together for the consolation of his heart—which desires unity in the body of Christ, on earth as it is in heaven!

Before we begin our pilgrimage of cultivating the unity that Jesus prayed for before he entered into his passion, I want to acknowledge that racial relations in the United States is a sensitive topic. It is easy to feel hurt, alienated, overwhelmed, and discouraged when considering this subject. It is also easy to become distracted by current social and political considerations. I want to invite you to read these pages with discernment and with an open mind and heart.

As a priest and author, I pray that my words in this book have been guided by the Holy Spirit. It goes without saying that they are not infallible. Therefore, I am open to any valid criticism and correction. It is not my intention to accuse, condemn, or discourage anyone with my words. Words of accusation, condemnation, and discouragement can be temptations from Satan, the father of lies. From the depths of my heart, I believe that we have an opportunity now to cast out the demonic stronghold of racism, which has divided and oppressed the Church in our nation for centuries. My hope is that you, the readers, are inspired by Jesus to be instruments of reformation and reconciliation in the racially divided body of Christ.

As you pray with the content provided in this book, please be aware that the enemy will seek to prevent you from participating in the work of racial reconciliation through lies and misunderstandings. I encourage you to receive the sacraments of the Eucharist and Reconciliation as often as possible so that the grace of God might be strengthened within you as you consider the challenges raised in these pages.

Here is a prayer of deliverance you can pray at the conclusion of each chapter so that you can remain open and receptive to every word that is from God, even if they are difficult. This prayer can also help you to avoid any suggestions the enemy might propose in his attempts to stop you from consoling the heart of Jesus in promoting unity in the divided body of Christ in our country.

Lord Jesus Christ, in your name and through your power, I ask that you pour forth your Precious Blood over me so that no demonic forces or strongholds may accuse, condemn, confuse, or discourage me with their lies. I ask that you bind any spirits of division, hatred, violence, indifference, and racism. Blessed Mother, Mary most holy, wrap me in your mantle of love. St. Joseph, terror of demons, surround me with your cloak of protection. St. Michael the Archangel, guard me with your shield so that I may remain fixed on the gaze of my heavenly Father who sees me, knows me, delights in me, loves me, and calls me by name to console the heart of Jesus by working for reformation and reconciliation in the racially divided body of Christ. Legions of angels under the command of the Blessed Virgin Mary, intercede for me so that I may be inspired and encouraged to imitate the apostles who received the Holy Spirit at Pentecost and went out to make disciples of all nations, races, tribes, and tongues. All you saints of heaven, plead before the throne of God for me, my family, my loved ones, and every member in the geographical boundaries of my parish that we may be protected from the snares of the enemy as we pray, fast, and work together to heal the racial divide in the United States of America.
Amen.

CHAPTER 1

Unity in the Mystical Body of Christ

"One thing have I asked of the LORD, that will I seek after; that I may dwell in the house of the LORD all the days of my life, to behold the beauty of the LORD, and to inquire in his temple."

— Psalm 27:4

Like me, have you ever wondered what heaven is like?

None of us, of course, knows what heaven looks like because we have not seen it. After all, as St. Paul reminds us, "no eye has seen, nor ear heard, nor the heart of man conceived, what God has prepared for those who love him" (1 Corinthians 2:9). We know, however, that we are called to set our hearts and minds on this eternal destination to which we have all been called (see Colossians 3:2).

Though "no eye has seen," can we know *anything* about what heaven is like?

Thankfully, at least one saint and mystic saw and wrote about heaven in Sacred Scripture, which means his words are part of the public revelation of the Church and "without error."[1] This man was one of the original twelve apostles, and he accompanied Jesus for three years. He was invited to climb the top of Mount Tabor, rest his head on the breast of Jesus at the Last Supper, pray with Jesus in the garden of Gethsemane, and was entrusted with the mother of Jesus at the foot of the Cross. The apostle I am referring to here is, of course, St. John, the Beloved Disciple and the author of the Gospel named after him and the book of Revelation.

Toward the end of his life, St. John experienced a mystical vision of heaven while in exile on the island of Patmos. He wrote about this mystical encounter in the book of Revelation. In richly symbolic language, St. John details who dwells in heaven and what the blessed "do" as they abide in the presence of the Living God:

> Behold, a great multitude which no man could number, from every nation, from all tribes and peoples and tongues, standing before the throne and before the Lamb, clothed in white robes, with palm branches in their hands, and crying out with a loud voice, "Salvation belongs to our God who sits upon the throne, and to the Lamb!" And all the angels stood round the throne and round the elders and the four living creatures, and they fell on their faces before the throne and worshiped God, saying, "Amen! Blessing and glory and wisdom and thanksgiving and honor and power and might be to our God for ever and ever! Amen." (Revelation 7:9-12)

When John was taken up into heaven, he saw God being worshipped by the choirs of angels and the saints. In heaven, all the focus is on God. There is no sadness, no sin, no brokenness. Because God is all in all, the angels and saints are completely happy.

When Jesus himself taught his disciples to pray, he included the words: "Thy kingdom come, thy will be done on earth as it is in heaven" (Matthew 6:10). While our time on earth is a time of pilgrimage, not the fullness of joy in heaven, we are called to know, love, and serve God here and not hold anything back.

The fullness of joy in heaven is important to keep in mind as we walk with Jesus Christ. I believe we become settled in our spiritual life because we think our current situation will never improve. We think it will continue in a downward spiral. As in "Murphy's Law," we think that everything that could go wrong, will go wrong. The same attitude can apply to our relationships with people. We settle for mediocrity or the status quo because we consider our possibilities limited or see our efforts showing little progress.

When we look at the kingdom of God on earth, particularly as it is reflected in the Church in America, what do we see? How closely does it resemble St. John's vision of heaven?

There are many ways we could answer this question. We could examine our commitment to prayer in our parishes, or the fervor of our ministry to the poor and needy.

However, I would like to point out something about St. John's vision of heaven that often goes unnoticed. The saints around the throne of God that St. John saw were people from every "nation," "tribe," and "tongue." The Greek word for nations is *ethnos*, from which the English word "ethnicity" is derived, and some biblical translations use the word "race" here. So he saw people of every race and ethnicity united in harmonious worship before the throne of God.

Do our small group Bible studies, RCIA programs, Adoration chapels, Sunday Masses, and parishes in America resemble St. John's vision of heaven in this way?

Every Tribe and Tongue

To help us consider where things stand, let's ask ourselves the following question: Does my parish intentionally invite people of every "tribe and tongue" to join in its worship of God at the holy sacrifice of the Mass, along with the choirs of angels and the multitude of saints in heaven?

Based on my own experience and the witness of others, I propose that many of our Catholic churches in America, even those located in diverse communities, do not resemble John's vision of heaven in the book of Revelation. As Rev. Dr. Martin Luther King Jr. stated in an April 17, 1960 interview on *Meet the Press*, "It is one of the tragedies of our nation, one of the shameful tragedies that eleven o'clock on Sunday morning is one of the most segregated hours, if not the most segregated hour in Christian America."[2]

Echoing Dr. Martin Luther King Jr.'s wisdom, I also believe that welcoming disciples from all nations, peoples, tribes, and tongues to the worship of God—specifically at the holy sacrifice of the Mass—is the foundational work that all practicing Catholics are being encouraged by our Lord to participate in as we accompany one another in our walk toward eternity. Communal prayer in the presence of the Eucharist has the power to transform and unite people of all nations.

Communal prayer in the presence of the Body, Blood, Soul, and Divinity of Jesus Christ in the Blessed Sacrament must be at the forefront of our minds because communal prayer was the first mandate Jesus Christ gave to his apostles after their ordination at the Last Supper. Before Jesus invited his apostles to teach, preach, heal, baptize, and disciple all of the nations, he invited them to spend time with him and each other in the practice of prayer. St. Matthew writes,

> Then Jesus went with them to a place called
> Gethsemane, and he said to his disciples, "Sit here,
> while I go over there and pray." And taking with
> him Peter and the two sons of Zebedee, he began to
> be sorrowful and troubled. Then he said to them ...
> "Watch and pray." (Matthew 26:36–38, 41)

Notice, the first task of disciples is to sit with Jesus, watch him, and pray. Once we are abiding together in relationship with God through our prayer and worship, we will have the grace that is necessary to go out into our wounded nation that has been divided by years of racist practices (unwritten rules) and policies (written rules) and transform our land into a just, hospitable, and charitable community as seen in Scripture in the ministry of the disciples in the early Church.

In the Acts of the Apostles, after the disciples were faithful to the first mandate of Christ to sit, watch, and pray, they were filled with the Holy Spirit and began to dwell in fellowship with disciples of every nation, people, tribe, and tongue. St. Luke writes,

> When the day of Pentecost had come, they were
> all together in one place. And suddenly a sound
> came from heaven like the rush of a mighty
> wind, and it filled all the house where they were
> sitting ... Now there were dwelling in Jerusalem
> Jews, devout men from every nation under heaven.
> And at this sound the multitude came together ...
> Parthians and Medes and Elamites and residents of
> Mesopotamia, Judea and Cappadocia, Pontus and
> Asia, Phrygia and Pamphylia, Egypt and the parts of
> Libya belonging to Cyrene, and visitors from Rome,
> both Jews and proselytes, Cretans and Arabians.
> (Acts 2:1–2, 5–6, 9–11)

Clearly, St. Luke's racially diverse description of the early Church mirrors St. John's vision of people from every nation, tribe, and tongue in heaven! The ethnic diversity of the early Church is also possible for our contemporary American Church.

Are you interested in discovering some of the reasons why the American Catholic Church does not currently look like the Church in heaven? Do you desire to learn how we can work together to reconcile the body of Christ on earth as it is in heaven? If so, I want to invite you to listen, learn, pray, and act so that we can be inspired by the same Holy Spirit who called the first disciples to abide in communion with people of every nation, tribe, and tongue on earth as it is in heaven!

CHAPTER 2

Invited into the Body of Christ

As I sat in the darkened chapel in quiet prayer, my eyes were drawn to the flickering candles on the altar. When I entered, there was no one else present. There was stillness and quiet, and I felt great joy and peace in the Eucharistic presence of Jesus.

This peaceful moment would not last long.

As I prayed, eyes closed, I heard someone come in and kneel down near me. Soon, I heard sobbing. When I turned to look, I saw that the man was a priest. I did not know what to do. So I asked Jesus, "Should I keep praying and just mind my own business? Should I intercede for him? Should I engage him and ask if I could help in any way?" After a few moments, I felt called to gently lean over and whisper, "Hey brother, I don't want to interrupt your time with Jesus, but is there anything I can do for you?" In between sobs, he shared that his superior had unexpectedly given him a new assignment, and he was devastated at where he was being sent—to a predominantly African American parish.

He told me, "I don't know why my superiors are sending me to a Black church. I don't know any Black people. I didn't grow up with Black people. How am I supposed to minister to them? What if I cannot preach the way they are used to? They are not going to accept me. They are not going to want me to be their priest!"

I was shocked by his words, and I was not sure how to respond. On a purely human level, my heart hurt to hear him express his sadness at his new assignment to serve African American Catholics. My father is Black, while my mother is white. Spiritually, though, I was grateful that this priest chose to go to this chapel to relate his fears and frustrations to Jesus. Pastorally, I did not know if I should chastise him or encourage him. Thanks be to God, I chose the latter.

While the exact details are not crystal clear, I do remember sharing that God speaks to us through our superiors, so I was certain that he had gifts that would help this predominantly African American community become the holy people God was calling them to be. I also shared that his new parishioners would help him grow in holiness. We then prayed together, and he left shortly thereafter.

Alone with Jesus again, my heart and mind went in many directions. I had trouble focusing on the Lord because my thoughts kept going back to the encounter with the priest. As St. Teresa of Avila teaches, for prayer to be authentic, we need to know the one to whom we are talking. We also need to know what, specifically, we are bringing to the Lord. So, when I am by myself, I find it helpful to speak out loud while praying. It helps me remain attentive to my dialogue with God.

While details are a bit hazy, my conversation with God went something like this:

"Does this man even know you, Lord? When he discerned his call to the priesthood, did he think he would only be serving people who look, think, and pray like him? Did he think his future parishioners would only come from the same socioeconomic background as him? Did he imagine that his priesthood would be spent exclusively serving Catholics of his race or ethnicity?"

I do not recall Jesus giving me any direct response to these questions. I do remember, though, that my time in prayer that day was more "wrestling" than it was praying.

Distance Caused by Lack of Relationship

Over the years, I have reflected on this experience and have come to realize the dangers of not interacting with people who are different from us—racially, ethnically, or socioeconomically. I do not assume this priest was racist simply because he was afraid to be assigned to a predominately African American parish. I do, however, believe his fear existed because he had had few, if any, intentional relationships with African Americans.*

Not long after my encounter with the distraught priest, I received my own new assignment. My bishop in the Diocese of Baton Rouge, Robert Muench, asked me to serve as pastor of Holy Rosary Church in St. Amant, Louisiana. While I was grieved at the thought of leaving the parishioners and students of St. Aloysius in Baton Rouge, I also felt excited as I thought about this new beginning as a pastor. I knew Holy Rosary faced some challenges. Among other things, it had been hit

---

* As I strive daily to understand more about the Lord's call to be an effective evangelist, there are a few words that have become part of my vocabulary that will be used throughout this book. One of these is "intentional." When I say that we need to have an intentional relationship with others, this means that these relationships must have purpose and meaning—that is, to be oriented toward something deeper than the current reality.

In the following pages, I will also use the phrase "*lean in.*" I love this phrase. Commonly used in the business world, it simply means to give something your complete focus—to make it a priority to the exclusion of other, less important realities.

by some recent catastrophic flooding. Thirteen people died, and hundreds of thousands were forced from their homes. There would be a lot of rebuilding to do in the community. Discerning this was God's plan for my ministry, though I was excited to enter into this new season of life.

When my peers heard the news about the assignment, they were less than excited for me. That particular town had a bad history in race relations. Many times I heard, "Josh, don't you realize that the Bayou Knights of the Ku Klux Klan were active in St. Amant?"

This was news to me. Being from Louisiana, I am familiar with overt racism, both in years past and even today. But I did not know the history of St. Amant, nor that of Holy Rosary parish. So I did what every young person does today—I went to Google.

I found a lot of information, and it was not pretty. I read articles that chronicled KKK rallies and acts of discrimination against African Americans in the early 2000s. I read of strife and division. So it seemed that what I had heard from my community was accurate.

Some of my friends advised me to request a different assignment from my bishop. One said, "You need to tell your bishop that you can't go to that town because that is a racist community, and you are the only African American priest in the diocese!" While these concerns were sincere, I did not share them. After all, I thought, just because a small group in the community publicly supports racist ideology does not mean that the parishioners of Holy Rosary are racist. If I immediately thought that they were racist simply because others in the community were, I would be stereotyping an entire group of people I had been asked to serve. I would be no different than the priest I had encountered who had stereotyped those African American Catholics he had been invited to serve.

The Problem with Stereotypes

Racial stereotypes can lead to prejudiced feelings about people we do not know, and prejudiced feelings can easily lead to discrimination. The anxiety of the priest I encountered in the chapel may have stemmed from stereotyped views rooted in his limited interaction with African Americans. If he had known and had relationships with Black people, his reaction to being assigned to a predominantly Black parish would more likely have been one of joy rather than fear.

Listening to the concerns expressed to me regarding St. Amant and its KKK connection, I reached out to Bishop Shelton Fabre of the nearby Diocese of Houma-Thibodaux. He is a personal friend and mentor who also happens to be African American. I knew he would be able to relate to my experience.

I shared with Bishop Fabre some of the concerns I was hearing about my parish assignment. He shared with me some wise words that I will never forget. "Josh," he said, "it's not so much about whether people accept you wherever you are assigned. It is more about whether you will accept them."

The good bishop's words gave me much comfort. I decided to *lean in* to my assignment and the people of this parish the best I could. I would seek to form an intentional relationship—a purposeful, meaningful relationship—with every member of Holy Rosary and the wider St. Amant community. I would commit to hearing their stories, praying with them, and inviting them to be intentional disciples of Jesus Christ. I would strive to walk with them toward eternity.

People Hungry for Jesus

As I began my assignment at Holy Rosary, I encountered a group of people who were already hungry for Jesus. They were eager to mature in discipleship. In time, I would have conversations with the parishioners about the history of their town of St. Amant. I would learn that the majority of them were extremely uncomfortable with the KKK's presence in their community and actively opposed its hateful ideology. Others, though, shared with me their past support of the KKK's ideology and racial segregation but had since repudiated these beliefs. Still others were indifferent to the entire issue. Regardless, I invited everyone to a deeper life in Christ, through the sacraments, Bible study, prayer, and fellowship.

Praised be to God, I witnessed much supernatural fruit from this simple act of inviting every person I met in my new community to "sit at the table of the Lord." Many who had been away from the Church returned to the sacraments, some discerned vocations to the religious life, others living in irregular marriages began working on getting their unions blessed by the Church, and still others stepped out of their own comfort zones and facilitated Bible studies in their homes and participated in works of charity and justice. The collective witness of these disciples of Jesus resulted in many people entering the Catholic Church through our parish's Rite of Christian Initiation of Adults (RCIA) program.

Distance Breeds Distrust and Fear

Over the past few years, I have spoken on the topic of racism and the racial division in the American Church today to thousands of Catholics. I have been invited to parishes, conferences, colleges, seminaries, high schools, diocesan summits, and gatherings of religious communities to speak on this issue. Interestingly, the majority of the attendees at these talks are white. I am absolutely seeing a sincere desire to advance racial harmony in the body of Christ. The means of this pursuit is through the proclamation of the gospel—that humanity fell, God came among us to save us, and we are called to build here on earth the glory that is found in heaven.

Even still, there is an underlying fear that accompanies this holy desire. Many who desire to seek out and cultivate relationships with those who are racially, ethnically, or socioeconomically different are hesitant. Why is this? I think it is because there is a natural distrust and fear that comes with "distance."

Speaking honestly, as I observe the actions of many lay and religious leaders of the Catholic Church in America, I see a lot of fear. This fear is not only rooted in the unknown but also in stereotypes. This fear leads to some pastors hesitating to walk closely—intentionally—with parishioners who are racially or ethnically different from them. It leads to only modest investment, at best, by many dioceses in serving predominantly Black communities.

In his program *Walking Toward Eternity: Engaging the Struggles of Your Heart*, Jeff Cavins describes fear as an acronym meaning "**f**alse **e**vidence **a**ppearing **r**eal."[3] This is what I think happens in the area of race relations—incomplete, or even false, evidence appearing as "real" and breeding distrust.

Distance amplifies this "false evidence" reality. When we have no relationship or experience with those who are different from us, we can easily believe false narratives about them. In my view, these false narratives have nearly paralyzed many Catholic leaders in the United States from sharing the gift of the Catholic Faith with every member of our community. As a result, many of our predominantly African American communities have been denied the greatest gift of all—the Body, Blood, Soul, and Divinity of Jesus in the sacrament of the Holy Eucharist. In fact, it is through sharing the Eucharist that the people of God achieve true unity in Christ.

As the Church teaches, the Eucharist is "the source and summit of the Christian life" (CCC 1324). The greatest saints were formed in the presence of the Eucharist. As St. Damien of Molokai, the missionary to the lepers in Hawaii, said, "Were it not for the constant presence of our Divine Master in our humble chapel, I would not be able to persevere in participating in the same fate as the lepers of Molokai ... the Eucharist is the bread of life that gives strength."[4] The great missionary to the poorest of the poor, St. Teresa of Calcutta (Mother Teresa), teaches, "The time that you spend with Jesus in the Blessed Sacrament is the best time you will spend on earth. Each moment that you spend with Jesus will deepen your union with him and make your soul everlastingly more glorious and beautiful in heaven."[5]

The Eucharist is the source and summit of our Faith, and "we who are many are one body, for we all partake of the one bread" (1 Corinthians 10:17). Despite this, it is my experience that many sincere Catholic ministers and laity are so afraid of saying or doing something wrong or unintentionally offending people of different races or ethnicities, that they end up doing little or nothing at all. Or they fear being misunderstood. Others believe they will not be able to relate to those of another race, and so the only intentional relationships they have are with people who look, think, and act like them.*

The net result of all this fear is that many people of color in the United States of America remain outside of the Catholic Church. We are not invited to participate in the sacramental life of the Church, nor are we engaged as essential members

---

* Some bishops have established "personal parishes" in their dioceses to accommodate communities drawn together by language, ethnicity, or liturgical rite. Such personal parishes have been helpful in fostering faith among those who have been marginalized by members of the geographic (or "territorial") parishes in which they reside. Regardless of whether we belong to a personal or a territorial parish, each of us is called to live out the Great Commission to "make disciples of all nations" in our community.

of the life-giving Church that Jesus himself established. This is a tragedy indeed.

I acknowledge that many affluent parishes have generous outreaches to low-income people of every race within their geographical boundaries. This is good. There is a greater good, however, that many of these parishes neglect—namely, the call of Jesus to invite all people, regardless of ethnicity or race, to that unparalleled relationship with him in the Eucharist.

Racial Division as a "Church Problem"

While sitting in a Birmingham, Alabama, jail cell in 1963, the Rev. Dr. Martin Luther King Jr. wrote his famous letter to the world. In it, he proclaimed that the division between Black and white people in American society was primarily a "church problem." I would take Dr. King's assessment a step further and propose that the racial divide in our nation is a "Eucharist problem."

Why do I say this? The words of St. Peter Julian Eymard are helpful here. Writing in the early 1900s, he notes that the Eucharist is the life of all nations; it forms a common bond for people from diverse nations and languages and brings them to the law of charity for and with each other:

> *All* eat of the same bread, all are Jesus Christ's guests, and he supernaturally forms among them a certain harmony of brotherly customs ... At the holy table, all are children taking the same food ... Therefore, the Eucharist imparts on the Christian community the power to preserve the law of honor and love of neighbor.[6]

It is a tragedy that racial division exists where there should no longer be any division—in the Eucharistic celebration of our communion in Jesus Christ. If the Eucharist gives us the power to maintain love between all people, then I propose the segregation at the Eucharistic table in most of our church parishes is one of the root causes of the disunity we see between Black and white people in our nation.

The African Catholic Heritage

The Church in Africa has been an evangelical force for Christianity for two thousand years. In fact, centuries before missionaries brought the Catholic Faith to the United States, the early Church disciples of Jesus planted Catholic communities in Africa. The African Catholic experience can be traced back to the Acts of the Apostles and the baptism of the Ethiopian eunuch by St. Philip the deacon. You might recall the story of Philip's journey from Jerusalem to Gaza through the desert and his encounter with the eunuch, who was a minister to Candace, the Ethiopian queen.

> Philip ... heard him reading Isaiah the prophet, and asked, "Do you understand what you are reading?" And he said, "How can I, unless some one guides me?" ... Then Philip opened his mouth, and beginning with this Scripture he told him the good news of Jesus. And as they went along the road they came to some water, and the eunuch said, "See, here is water! What is to prevent my being baptized?" And he commanded the chariot to stop, and they both went down into the water, Philip and the eunuch, and he baptized him. And when they came up out of the water, the Spirit of the Lord caught up Philip; and the eunuch saw him no more, and went on his way rejoicing. (Acts 8:30–31, 35–39)

The African Church would grow quickly and, in time, produce three popes: Pope Victor I in 189, Pope Miltiades in 311, and Pope Gelasius in 492. Many canonized saints have come out of Africa, including Saints Ambrose, Augustine, Monica, Perpetua, Felicity, Benedict the Moor, Mary of Egypt, Charles Lwanga and the Ugandan Martyrs, and Josephine Bakhita. The list is a long one.

One of the greatest African saints was a fourth-century monk who came to be known as St. Moses the Black. In his early life, he was an outlaw and alleged murderer. The exact circumstances surrounding his conversion are unknown, but, at some point, he encountered the love of Christ and became a monk and eventually a priest. In the early Church, it was unusual for a monk to be ordained a priest, so this was a rare honor. He would become the leader of a small group of hermits in the western desert of Egypt. Around the year 405, at the age of seventy-five, Moses and his fellow hermits were martyred by the Berbers because of their commitment to Christ. To this day, monks continue to be inspired by the example of St. Moses the Black.[7]

In the present day, the Christian community in Africa is bearing great spiritual fruit. Holy bishops, priests, and lay leaders are forming many intentional disciples of Jesus and leading them into the sacramental life of the Catholic Church. Currently, there are over 135 million Catholics on the continent of Africa. In 2015, a crowd of thirty thousand attended the beatification of Blessed Benedict Daswa (1946–1990), a South African teacher who was martyred in 1990 by an anti-Christian mob because of his fidelity to Jesus and his teachings.

Shaking Up the Status Quo

The Catholic Church in America will not bear the kind of supernatural fruit the Church in Africa is witnessing unless we shake up the status quo.

How do we do this? We need to dispel the misunderstanding and overcome the fears that some Catholics have, consciously or unconsciously, about people from different races or ethnicities. These fears keep us from joining together at the Eucharistic table.

As St. John reminds us, "Perfect love casts out fear" (1 John 4:18). If we simply *lean in* to Jesus, who is Love, he will cast out all fear and give us the grace needed to imitate him and cross cultural boundaries. We will then invite everyone, regardless of race or ethnicity, to be united at the Eucharistic banquet of the Church. We will see and engage each other as disciples of Christ.

Currently, there are six African American Catholics who are on the path to becoming canonized saints: Pierre Toussaint, Julia Greely, Fr. Augustus Tolton, Sister Thea Bowman, Mother Mary Elizabeth Lange, and Mother Henriette Delille. All six of these holy men and women were accompanied by some white Catholics who, following the model of Jesus, saw them as brothers and sisters in Christ. This said, these six future saints also suffered persecution at the hands of many white leaders in the Church. With all my heart, I believe that one of the reasons why the United States of America has so few canonized saints from our nation is because so many Catholics have historically participated in sins of racism, whether by omission or commission. All of us are called to image the harmony and unity of the Church in heaven while we are here on earth.

The Power of Fasting

As you read along, I invite you to the ascetical practice of fasting. Fasting is one of the first commandments that God gave to Adam and Eve in the Garden of Eden. Concerning the Tree of the Knowledge of Good and Evil, God said, "You shall not eat" (Genesis 2:17). In addition to God commanding our first parents to fast in the Garden, our Blessed Mother, the Virgin Mary, has also been inviting Catholics to fast in her many apparitions all over the world, including Kibeho in Africa, Fatima in Europe, and Akita in Asia. Traditionally, fasting involves restricting the amount of food we eat so we can discipline our bodies in imitation of Jesus in his passion. Fasting reminds us that conversion must touch our bodies as well as our souls. When we fast, it is also fruitful to spend some focused time with Sacred Scripture so that the Word of God can penetrate our hearts, minds, and actions.

St. John Chrysostom, a fourth-century Church Father, invites us to fast not only from food, but also from attitudes, thoughts, and sinful desires:

> He who limits his fasting only to an abstinence from meats, is one who especially disparages it. Dost thou fast? Give me proof of it by thy works! Is it said by what kind of works? If thou seest a poor man, take pity on him! If thou seest an enemy, be reconciled to him! If thou seest a friend gaining honour, envy him not! ... For let not the mouth only fast, but also the eye, and the ear, and the feet, and the hands, and all the members of our bodies. Let the hands fast, by being pure from rapine and avarice. Let the feet fast, by ceasing from running to the unlawful spectacles. Let the eyes fast, being taught never to fix themselves rudely upon handsome countenances, or to busy themselves with strange beauties. For looking is the food of the eyes, but if this be such as is unlawful or forbidden, it mars the fast; and upsets the whole safety of the soul; but if it be lawful and safe, it adorns fasting. For it would be among things the most absurd to abstain from lawful food because of the fast, but with the eyes to touch even what is forbidden.[8]

I invite you to practice fasting as you read this book. I also encourage you to *lean in* to praying with God's teachings, as given to us in the Scriptures and the *Catechism of the Catholic Church*. One powerful approach is the ancient practice of *lectio divina* or "divine reading" (CCC 2708), which enables us to take a particular Bible passage or teaching from the *Catechism* and enter more deeply into their mystery and meaning.

Traditionally, *lectio divina* has four steps:

- **Step 1: Reading**
  Here, one simply slowly and attentively reads the words of the text, nothing more. The goal of this first step is to understand the plain meaning of what we are reading.

- **Step 2: Meditation**
  Meditate on the words you have read, seeking to discover what they are saying to you now.

- **Step 3: Prayer**
  Reach out to God in prayer, conversing with him through the Holy Spirit, using the text you have just meditated upon.

- **Step 4: Contemplation**
  If you are praying before Jesus in the Blessed Sacrament, allow yourself to abide with him and experience the "gaze" of God as you adore him in the Eucharist. If you are praying outside of Eucharistic Adoration, allow yourself to "rest" in the Lord, silently focusing your mind and heart on him.

As we spend time with Jesus, he equips us as his disciples with the tools that help us to cross cultural lines. Our goal is to cultivate dialogue with all believers so we can "make disciples of all nations" (Matthew 28:19) and so we can bring about the unity for which Jesus prayed (see John 17:21). It is the Lord's desire that the Church on earth reflect the diversity of the Church in heaven, where we will all gather at the table in peace and harmony.

CHAPTER 3

Imitating the Body of Christ

Once, a journalist asked a priest this question: "Who is Jesus Christ for you?" The priest was Fr. Pedro Arrupe, who served as the superior general of the Society of Jesus (the Jesuits) from 1965 to 1983. In response to the journalist's question, Fr. Arrupe declared, "For me, Jesus Christ is everything!"

Fr. Arrupe was on fire with love for Jesus. In the words of a popular meditation that is often attributed to him,

> Nothing is more practical than finding God, that is, than falling in love in a quite absolute, final way. What you are in love with, what seizes your imagination, will affect everything. It will decide what will get you out of bed in the morning, what you do with your evenings, how you spend your weekends, what you read, whom you know, what breaks your heart, and what amazes you with joy and gratitude. Fall in love, stay in love, and it will decide everything.[9]

A few years after I had come to a deep love for Jesus through the time I spent with him in Eucharistic Adoration, I discerned a call to the priesthood and entered St. Joseph's Abbey and Seminary College in Covington, Louisiana. After graduating from St. Joseph's Seminary with a bachelor's degree in liberal arts and philosophy, I began my studies at Notre Dame Graduate School of Theology in New Orleans.

Called to Serve ... Everyone

In my third year of theological studies, a new rector was named to Notre Dame, Fr. Jim Wehner. This holy man had served as a priest of the Diocese of Pittsburgh since his ordination in 1995 and brought many years of pastoral wisdom with him to our Louisiana seminary. One of the principles that Fr. Wehner emphasized constantly was the responsibility of the pastor for every person in the geographical boundaries of his parish. This is a message that my brother priests and I need to keep in mind. We are called to serve not merely the baptized and registered Catholics in our parish but everyone who lives in our community.

Yes, as pastors, we clearly must pray, teach, serve, and even fast for the parishioners we see before us at Mass every Sunday. But we are also duty bound to share Jesus with all people who live in our parish, regardless of their religion, race, ethnicity, gender, age, sexual preference, political ideology, or socioeconomic background. I believe we will actually be held accountable by God on our judgment day for how we sought to minister to each soul in our community. Before the Lord in prayer, we need to consider the following question: To the best of our ability and opportunity, are we wholeheartedly seeking to invite every person living within our parish boundaries to encounter Jesus Christ and have a relationship with him in the sacraments?

The Witness of Sister Teresa Berlin

One modern-day disciple of Jesus who is intentional with every person in her community is a hermit nun named Sister Teresa Berlin. She and I became friends during my studies at St. Joseph's Seminary College. Sister Teresa spent many years as a cloistered nun with the Poor Clares of Perpetual Adoration with EWTN founder Mother Angelica. After years of adoring Jesus in the Blessed Sacrament with this community of holy sisters, she discerned a call from Jesus to leave the cloister and live out her religious life as a hermit in Covington, Louisiana.

Mother Angelica gave Sister Teresa permission to leave the cloister to better discern this potential new path. So, donned in her full Franciscan habit, Teresa began to live out her new vocation in a small hermitage in Covington, Louisiana. The majority of her day was spent with the Sacred Scriptures and in the Presence of Christ in the Blessed Sacrament. Daily, visitors would stop by to visit with her. In return, she offered them hospitality and love, seeking to draw them into a deeper relationship with Jesus.

The more time Sister Teresa spent praying before the Holy Eucharist, the more she began to think with the mind of Christ. There is a well-known spiritual adage that "adoration leads to imitation," and Sister Teresa began to perceive an invitation to imitate Jesus by seeking an intentional relationship with the poor of her community. She began to spend intentional time every week in a low-income, predominantly African American neighborhood, visiting with the men and women who were sitting on their porches and praying with them.

During her weekly "porch visits," she shared whatever food she had with her, usually fruit and vegetables. The people would share food with her as well. Sister Teresa talked to them about their lives and listened to their stories. She related her own story of how she fell in love with Jesus. She would invite them to pray with her so that they too could draw closer to the Lord.

While Sister Teresa was committed to spending intentional, consistent time with Jesus each day in the Scriptures and the

Eucharist, she was also committed to that same intentionality with him through her engagement with the people in this community.

With funds provided by Mother Angelica, Sister Teresa purchased an abandoned shack in the heart of the neighborhood. She immediately began renovating it so it could become a place for the elderly in the community to rest, enjoy fellowship, and pray. As it turned out, however, most who stopped by her little shack were neighborhood kids more than the older folks. Kids would visit her after school, and she would teach them songs and tell them stories about Jesus. She gave them a safe place where they could spend time together and grow in their relationship with each other.

Along with some adults in the neighborhood, Sister Teresa would take the children on road trips to visit parks for fun and area parishes for prayer. During these visits, she would always be sure to introduce them to Jesus in the Blessed Sacrament, and on the way, she would pray the Liturgy of the Hours with them. She listened with joy as the kids rapped, not chanted, the Psalms. She invited those who had not been baptized to do so. She longed for them to receive Jesus in the Holy Eucharist. As the children came to a deeper relationship with Christ through the sacraments, a number of the kids' parents returned to their practice of the Catholic Faith or came into the Church for the first time.

Not only did Sister Teresa experience great joy as she accompanied people into the sacramental life of the Church, but her witness also inspired one woman, Damika Jerry, to enter the Sisters of the Holy Family in New Orleans, a historically African American religious community. One day in prayer, Damika perceived the voice of Venerable Mother Henriette Delille, the founder of the Holy Family Sisters, inviting her to join the community. Today, Damika is known as Sister Marie Elizabeth, the same name Sister Teresa was given when she first professed herself as a Poor Clare sister. Not only does she bear the same name as her spiritual mother, but she also works with children as a religious sister, just like Sister Teresa.

The Need for Intentional Relationship

Inspired by Sister Teresa's ministry, I felt called to do similar work shortly after I was ordained to the priesthood. One of my first assignments was at an affluent parish in suburban Baton Rouge filled with many people who were striving to be intentional disciples of Jesus. Most of the parishioners at St. Aloysius Catholic Church were middle-class and upper-class white people. The parish's geographical boundaries, however, included people from diverse racial and economic backgrounds. Because of a Federal Housing Administration (FHA) policy in place from 1934 to 1977, some of the parish's neighborhoods were segregated by color since the FHA officially encouraged "redlining" and refused to insure mortgages for African Americans during this period. Though this policy has long since ended, its legacy endures in the form of socioeconomic, rather than legal, segregation.[10]

A predominantly low-income Black neighborhood was located just five minutes from the parish church. In fact, many of my friends from high school lived in this neighborhood. At a certain point after being assigned to the parish, I began walking the streets as I prayed the Rosary. I would frequently encounter former classmates. Although I also did these same "Rosary walks" in the more affluent and predominantly white neighborhoods of my parish, an unsettling conversation with an old friend from high school caused me to focus most of my efforts in the low-income, predominantly Black area.

The conversation happened with a woman named Traci, who I had last spoken with at my ordination. She asked me why I was walking through the neighborhood, and I explained that I had been assigned to St. Aloysius. She looked at me with a peculiar expression and said, "Huh. I didn't even know there was a Catholic Church across the tracks." I was shocked. Traci had lived in this neighborhood her entire life, and yet she had never even heard about this large, vibrant parish. In fact, some of the more affluent parishioners had even provided financial assistance to refugee families in the neighborhood for scholarships at the parish school. The parish was also present in the neighborhood through its St. Vincent de Paul Society, communion visits to the homebound, and financial support of the neighborhood grocery store. Even with all these good works, something critical was missing. It was clear that we needed to do much more to reach out to the poorer neighborhoods of the parish to invite all people into the sacramental life of our community.

During my Rosary walks, I would greet and speak with anyone I encountered. Because I was in clerical attire, people were usually open to talking to me about God, and I used the opportunity to invite them to spend time at the church. I would soon see, though, that my walks through the neighborhood were not going unnoticed by some of the parishioners of St. Aloysius.

Once, a parishioner who was active in the church asked me in an accusatory tone, "Why do you keep going to 'that' neighborhood?" I responded that, according to the canon law of the Church, I was responsible for ministering to every person within the parish boundaries, regardless of race, religion, or background. I emphasized the importance of making all people feel welcome in the Church, including those from "that" neighborhood.

Not satisfied with my answer, she said, "But Father, why do they have to come here? We've already given many of those people money through our St. Vincent de Paul ministry. Don't they have their own churches to attend?"

Shocked by this visceral response, I tried gently to shift her viewpoint: "Don't you realize that those people are made in the image and likeness of God and that they belong to this parish as much as you do? Many of them have never been introduced to Jesus in the Holy Eucharist. Jesus said that those who eat the Bread of Life will have eternal life. Do you want those people to have eternal life or not?"

At that point, she looked at me thoughtfully for a moment, then leaned in and said in a low voice, "Listen, I just think you need to slow down a little. People don't like a lot of change."

True Discipleship

It goes without saying that this woman's attitude did not fit with the model of discipleship Jesus gives us in the Scriptures. While she did not mind financially supporting underprivileged African Americans in the parish through various outreaches, she kept her distance. She showed little desire to engage personally with the low-income African Americans in our parish's geographical boundaries. She was OK with providing them with food and financial support—as long as they stayed "over there" and stayed away from the church campus.

Over the years, I have met many who want to help the less fortunate with food for the body but not with the food for the soul, the Eucharist, which is the very means through which Jesus unites us in his body, the Church.

Many Catholic parishes are located in communities of color, yet the people sitting in the pews every Sunday are nearly all white. Unfortunately, some priests, deacons, religious sisters, lay directors of faith formation, and youth ministers have chosen to not go out into the predominantly Black neighborhoods of their parish and invite the people in their land to join a Bible study, attend an RCIA class, or get plugged into one of the parish's ministries.

Sharing the Gift

If we have been given a gift, the natural response is to be thankful for that gift and then share it with others. If the gift was given to us by someone really important, such as the president of the United States or the queen of England, we would likely share it with everyone we know. As Catholics, we have received gifts that are far better than those given by presidents or queens. We have been given the Bible and the sacraments, the greatest of these being the very Body and Blood of Jesus in the Eucharist. If we really believed this truth, we would want everyone in our parish's boundaries to participate in Mass and adore Jesus in the Blessed Sacrament. If we really believe that the Bible is the written word of God, then how can we not want to share its truth with everyone in our parish?

Color-Blind?

You will sometimes hear some well-intentioned Catholic leaders proclaim that they are "color-blind." While this might sound enlightened, this mindset can actually have a negative effect on their ministry. If one is blind to color, he or she could easily fail to notice just how few people of color are sitting in the pews at Mass every Sunday. They will be unaware of the pressing need to invite African Americans and other people of color who reside in their parish to a seat at the table because they simply do not "see" them.

Not long ago, a friend of mine attended a diocesan meeting for priests in which a consulting company presented demographic information about the people within the diocese's boundaries. The consultant showed charts to the people at the meeting describing what percentage of the diocese was white, Latino, and other. After a time, my friend began to notice something missing. The discussion of the racial backgrounds within the diocese did not mention Black people, although millions of Americans are Black—in 2019, 46.8 million people or fourteen percent of the population, in fact, according to Pew.[11] My friend raised his hand and asked why there was no mention of African Americans. The reply was unsettling. "They're in the 'other' category," the consultant told him.

A colorblind approach can leave Black people hidden from sight—as "other." When we within the Church are blind to the absence of others, we do not see those we are called to accompany in their walk toward eternity.

In my experience, there is a noticeable difference between most Catholic parishes and most evangelical Christian communities in the area of discipleship. On the whole, evangelical ministers are expected to go out into their geographical boundaries and meet people, one-on-one, and invite them into a personal relationship with Jesus. They have a clear "growth" mindset, and this usually carries over to the people in their pews. Catholic priests, by contrast, are usually assigned to well-established parishes that have typically been in existence for many years before they arrived. Some of these parishes were established to serve a specific ethnic group. This "established culture" can easily lead priests and parish leaders to focus just on the people who are already sitting in the pews—that is, on those who are already active in the parish.

In all honesty, I have fallen into this myself. At times, I have not been as zealous as I could have been in reaching out to those in my parish boundaries and inviting them into a personal relationship with Jesus in the sacraments.

As a new pastor at Holy Rosary, I inherited a community devastated in 2016 by a major flood in which thirteen people had died and thousands were displaced. At the time my assignment began, many were moving back into their homes, and businesses had started to reopen. This presented me with a unique opportunity of blessing homes and businesses. I started to do this each week. During these visits, I would sit with my parishioners and hear their thoughts, concerns, and hopes about the parish and its mission. One theme I heard often was a longing to help the less fortunate in our community since so many were in need due to the flood.

One of the buildings on our campus that was destroyed in the flood was an old rectory and office space. After prayerfully reflecting on the stories I heard, my team and I decided to restore and renovate this space and make it an outreach to the poorest of the poor in our community. In time, it would become a one-stop shop servicing many needs: a food pantry, coffee shop and cafe, soup kitchen, a barbershop and salon, and a diaper bank. It would house fertility care specialists (equipped with an ultrasound machine), lawyers, counselors, pharmacists, human resource directors, and academic tutors. It would also be a place for intentional fellowship, praise and worship, and small group Bible studies.

As we began the restoration process, a devout man heard about our plans and sent us a team of construction workers who almost completely renovated the space for a modest price. All of these workers were from Mexico or of Mexican descent. The foreman was a joyful man named Carlos. He was bilingual, but most of his co-workers only spoke Spanish. Unfortunately, I only knew a few phrases in Spanish. I would invite them to Mass and confession as best as I could. Looking back on my time with this crew of workers, I wish I would have invested more of my time learning their language. If I had been more intentional with language, then I could have potentially crossed some of our cultural boundaries in my efforts to share the joy of the gospel.

Going to the "Other Side of the Tracks" to Know Jesus

Jesus crossed cultural boundaries in his journey to Jerusalem. He shared hearts with the Samaritan woman at the well, he healed the servant of the Roman centurion, he ate with a tax collector (Matthew) who he called to become an apostle, and he invited children to become disciples. He addressed everyone, regardless of their status in life. This is the model of radical discipleship I need to follow. It is the model we all need to follow as followers of Christ.

There is a well-known adage that I believe is true: Many Catholics and other Christians know *about* Jesus ... but we do not *know* Jesus. It is possible for a Catholic to have received the sacraments and attend Catholic schools or religious education classes for many years, and yet still not really know Jesus. We may listen to Christian podcasts, read books on evangelization, catechesis, and apologetics, participate in retreats and conferences, and be engaged in acts of service to others and still not know the Lord. Our faith is simply in our head rather than our heart; it does not manifest itself in love toward our fellow men and women.

Commenting on the need for each of us to really know Jesus, St. Teresa of Calcutta addressed the sisters of her community, the Missionaries of Charity, with the following words:

> I worry some of you still have not really met Jesus—
> one to one—you and Jesus alone. We may spend time
> in chapel—but have you seen with the eyes of your
> soul how He looks at you with love? Do you really
> know the living Jesus—not from books, but from
> being with Him in your heart? Have you heard the
> loving words He speaks to you? Ask for the grace;
> He is longing to give it.[12]

So I ask you now: Do you know Jesus? Have you heard his voice in the quiet of prayer, urging you to a deeper relationship with him? Have you ever felt him looking at you with love? If not, then we need to ask him for the grace to do so. I have found that the more time I spend with Jesus in prayer, the more I experience who he is—my brother and my God. This then prompts me to want to imitate him in my life and ministry.

The best way that any of us can get to know Jesus is by setting time aside every day to meet him in Sacred Scripture. The great Catholic biblical scholar St. Jerome proclaimed in the fourth century that "ignorance of Scripture is ignorance of Christ." If we want to know Jesus, we must be intentional about knowing him. To begin, we should spend time reading about him in the Bible. As Orthodox priest and theologian Fr. Tom Hopko so eloquently says,

> The holy Scriptures—what can I say? We have to
> read them, contemplate them and put them into
> practice more than we breathe. It's terrible that we
> like spirituality books, read books on theology and
> the saints and holy Fathers, but we don't even know
> the holy Scriptures. That's not right! All of the holy
> Fathers say everything in the Christian life has its
> foundation on the canonized Scriptures of the Church
> ... The holy Scriptures should be our first love.[13]

As we begin our journey of abiding with God in the Bible, we will open our hearts and listen to him speak to us. We will see what Jesus wants to say to us today. In fact, they are the same words he said two thousand years ago to the original disciples: "Go therefore and make disciples of all nations" (Matthew 28:19). This is not merely a suggestion; it is a command from Jesus to anyone who would be his disciple. Clearly, the apostles fulfilled the demands of discipleship because they indeed went out and made disciples of all nations by evangelizing the world.

How to "Make Disciples of All Nations"

In the book of Acts, the apostles were gathered together with Mary on the day of Pentecost. Upon receiving the Holy Spirit, they went out and preached the gospel, first to the pilgrims gathered in Jerusalem for the feast.

> [The apostles] were filled with the Holy Spirit and began to speak in other tongues, as the Spirit gave them utterance. Now there were dwelling in Jerusalem Jews, devout men from every nation under heaven. And at this sound the multitude came together, and they were bewildered, because each one heard them speaking in his own language. (Acts 2:4-6)

Soon, they would spread the gospel to the rest of Israel, Asia Minor, Rome, and ultimately to the entire world. This required them to cross cultural boundaries—to reach out to people who looked, spoke, and thought differently from them. When we obey the command of Christ to "teach all nations," the supernatural fruit of leading all people, regardless of race or ethnicity, is the formation of saints. In the book of Revelation, St. John describes the supernatural fruit of this evangelization:

> Behold, a great multitude which no man could number, from every nation, from all tribes and peoples and tongues, standing before the throne and before the Lamb, clothed in white robes, with palm branches in their hands. (Revelation 7:9)

Just as the Father sent Jesus into the world, our Lord sends us into the world (see John 17:18). If, like the apostles, we heed his words in Scripture and seek to make disciples of all nations, we are seeking to make earth resemble heaven—with people of "every nation ... all tribes and peoples" united in Christ.

Putting on the Mind of Christ

Since it is the will of Christ that our churches on earth reflect the Church in heaven, the devil and his minions will seek to turn us away from our efforts at deeper discipleship. As the first letter of Peter tells us, "Your adversary the devil prowls around like a roaring lion, seeking some one to devour" (1 Peter 5:8).

Let us recall the very first temptation of Satan against humanity. In the Garden of Eden, Adam and Eve were united in communion with God and one another. Seeking to preserve their innocence, God commanded them not to eat the fruit of the Tree of the Knowledge of Good and Evil. At a certain point, Satan entered the garden and engaged Eve in a conversation. He asked her, "Did God say, 'You shall not eat of any tree of the Garden?'" (Genesis 3:1). Notice, this first temptation of the devil is for Eve to question what God had clearly commanded, to get her to doubt the goodness of his will.

Similarly, Satan tempts us to doubt what the Lord has communicated in the Gospels. His temptation goes something like this: *Did God really say that you are to make disciples of all nations? He surely cannot mean that literally. He just wants you to make disciples of some nations, those with whom you have something in common and can relate to. He just wants you to make disciples of people who look like you, speak your language, and have a similar socioeconomic background. You really don't need to go out of your comfort zone and cross cultural barriers. That would be asking too much.*

The devil wants us to be "cafeteria Catholics," picking and choosing the words of Jesus we will adhere to and dismissing other commands as too "idealistic" or "impractical." But the intentional Catholic is called to more than this—much more.

In the end, the aim of the devil is for us to think with the "mind of the world" and avoid going beyond what is comfortable in our walk with Jesus. As Catholics, though, we are exhorted by St. Paul to put on the mind of Christ (see Philippians 2:5)—who calls all people to enjoy the fruits of his love and salvation in his Church.

To put on the mind of Christ, we need to "fast from distractions" and prioritize intentional time with Sacred Scriptures, in Eucharistic Adoration, and in living a sacramental life. The more time we spend with Jesus, the more open we will be to thinking with his mind, seeing with his eyes, listening with his ears, speaking with his voice, walking with his feet, and working with his hands—all toward the bold and glorious end of making disciples of all nations.

CHAPTER 4

Listening to the Body of Christ

While speaking to the parishioners of All Saints Church in Pasadena, California, social psychologist and theologian Dr. Christena Cleveland offered a moving testimony of the good works God can do when disciples of Jesus break out of their "holy huddles" and enter into deep relationships with people from diverse backgrounds. She shared the story of a group of twenty-five women of European descent who were part of a prayer group and wanted to invite Latina mothers from the school where all of their children attended. Their efforts initially failed, but they were persistent. They reached out to Dr. Cleveland, who is often sought out by church leaders to share her insights on racial reconciliation, for a new approach.

After hearing about their failed attempts to include the Latina women, Dr. Cleveland asked when and where their prayer group met. They said they met on Thursday mornings at eleven o'clock in one of their homes. She then asked them, "Do you think there is any reason meeting at eleven o'clock on a Thursday morning might be an issue for the Latina ladies you invited?" The ladies responded, "We don't know."

Dr. Cleveland encouraged the group to find out by getting to know the Latina mothers through spending time in places and spaces that they frequented. The women agreed and began to attend prayer services with the Latina mothers at their Spanish-speaking ecclesial community.

After getting to know a few of the Latina mothers, they inquired why none came to their Thursday morning prayer group. The Latina women explained that, while they would very much like to be a part of this prayer group, they had to work—often more than one job—to help provide for their families. They were simply not able to attend during the middle of a workday.

When an evening meeting time was suggested, the Latina women explained that this would not work either as they used public transportation and got home late from work. They then suggested meeting in one of the Latina mother's homes. Everyone agreed this just might be the solution.

At the beginning, the prayer group had approximately twenty-five mothers of European descent and twenty Latina mothers. In time, the group would grow larger. The Latina moms shared that there were other moms in the neighborhood who wanted to join the group, but they did not speak English. A translator was hired, and several more joined the group. Eventually, twelve of the moms from the original prayer group learned Spanish so they could communicate better with the group's Spanish-speaking members.

As the women continued to spend time together, a trust was established between them. The women from both communities began to share their hearts with each other on a deeper level. The Latina women opened up about their struggles with some of the institutional practices (unwritten rules) and policies (written rules) that negatively affected their families. Their sisters in Christ listened to their stories, believed them, prayed with them, and began working with them to change the practices and policies in their communities.

These women emulated Pope Francis' invitation to every disciple of Jesus in his encyclical *Evangelii Gaudium* ("The Joy of the Gospel"):

> An evangelizing community gets involved by word and deed in people's daily lives; it bridges distances, it is willing to abase itself if necessary, and it embraces human life, touching the suffering flesh of Christ in others. Evangelizers thus take on the "smell of the sheep" and the sheep are willing to hear their voice.[14]

Likewise, as St. Paul writes in his first letter to the church in Thessalonica: "We were ready to share with you not only the gospel of God but also our own selves, because you had become very dear to us" (1 Thessalonians 2:8). Notice that St. Paul not only shared the gospel with these men and women, but he also shared his life with those he accompanied in discipleship. This is the model used by Jesus

An Active Seeking

Throughout his earthly life, Jesus cultivated intentional relationships in small groups. For his first thirty years on earth, he shared his life with his mother and father—the Holy Family—and he did so on their terms. He did not force Mary to be his mother. He went to her, through an angel, and proposed that she allow him into her life through the mystery of the Incarnation. He then intentionally submitted to Mary and St. Joseph as an obedient son (see Luke 2:51).

When he was ready to begin his public ministry, he did not wait for his disciples to come to him but went out to seek them where they were. The Gospel of Matthew reveals how Jesus invited Simon, soon to be St. Peter, to be his disciple:

> As he walked by the Sea of Galilee, he saw two brothers, Simon who is called Peter and Andrew his brother, casting a net into the sea; for they were fishermen. And he said to them, "Follow me, and I will make you fishers of men." Immediately they left their nets and followed him. And going on from there he saw two other brothers, James the son of Zebedee and John his brother, in the boat with Zebedee their father, mending their nets, and he called them. Immediately they left the boat and their father, and followed him. (Matthew 4:18-22)

Throughout his journey toward Jerusalem, Jesus went out to meet people and personally invite them to abide with him as a community of disciples. When people began to walk with Jesus, they prayed together, traveled together, shared meals, and attended celebrations together, such as the wedding feast of Cana. This should be our model for discipleship as well—to go out and meet people where they are and personally invite them to abide with us in prayer, Bible study, fellowship, the sacraments, and in outreach to the sick, suffering, and the most vulnerable in our community.

Again, Jesus did not sit around passively waiting for people to come to him. He went out and engaged everyone he met, listened to their stories, and shared the gospel in a way they could receive based on where they were at in that moment of their lives. While there are many examples of this in the Gospels, one that stands out is the story of when the Samaritan woman met Jesus at the well.

The Woman at the Well

On one of his journeys to Galilee, Jesus traveled through Samaria. Interestingly, he did not need to go through Samaria;

he could have taken a different route. As Craig Keener points out in his commentary *The Gospel of John*, Jesus did not seem to be in any particular hurry to get to Galilee. A closer examination of the narrative shows that the necessity that compels Jesus to take that route is probably his mission to bring the people of Samaria into a correct worship of God.[15]

To foster discipleship among the Samaritans, Jesus went to one of their wells, a place where people naturally gathered, at the "sixth hour"—that is, noon (see John 4:6). In a desert climate, this was the hottest time of the day, so many would avoid going out at that time. The fact that this particular woman chose to go to the well at noon indicates she wanted to go when there were few others present due to her reputation in the community.

When Jesus engaged her in dialogue, she was resistant because of their religious differences—he a Jew, she a Samaritan. Instead of talking religion with her, he paid attention to her circumstances, focusing on her needs at the present moment. He noticed that she was physically thirsty and that she was getting water at the hottest time of the day. We can assume Jesus knew that her choice to get water then indicated she was struggling with rejection from the community.

In this Gospel account, we see that the Samaritan woman was amazed when Jesus told her about her own life and her sins. Jesus invited her to let go of her unhealthy idols so that she could be open to receive the living water he would give her. In receiving his unconditional love, her thirst would be fully quenched.

Jesus went out of his way to meet her and listen to her heart. He communicated the gospel in a way that she could receive. Not only did she become a disciple, but she also went out into her community and invited them to a relationship with Jesus as well. In the Gospel of John, we read about how she left her water jar and went back to the city, saying to the people,

> "Come, see a man who told me all that I ever did. Can this be the Christ?" They went out of the city and were coming to him ... Many Samaritans from that city believed in him because of the woman's testimony, "He told me all that I ever did." So when the Samaritans came to him, they asked him to stay with them; and he stayed there two days. And many more believed because of his word. They said to the woman, "It is no longer because of your words that we believe, for we have heard for ourselves, and we know that this is indeed the Savior of the world." (John 4:29–30, 39–42)

Following this example, Jesus' followers also paid attention to the environment of the people they encountered. Like Jesus, they went out of their way and did whatever they could to invite people to a relationship with the living God. In the Gospel of Mark, we see how the apostles went to great lengths to assist a paralyzed man in his quest to be healed by Jesus:

> When [Jesus] returned to Capernaum after some days, it was reported that he was at home. And many were gathered together, so that there was no longer room for them, not even about the door; and he was preaching the word to them. And they came, bringing to him a paralytic carried by four men. And when they could not get near him because of the crowd, they removed the roof above him; and when they had made an opening, they let down the pallet on which the paralytic lay. And when Jesus saw their faith, he said to the paralytic, "Child, your sins are forgiven." (Mark 2:1–5)

This is the model of discipleship that, in my experience, has been missing in many parishes and dioceses in the United States. To better accompany every person who lives in the geographical boundaries of the parish, practicing Catholics are invited to go out and meet their neighbors, listen to their stories, pray with them, and discern together how they can best accompany each other in their relationship with Christ and the Church.

Breaking Out of Our Cultural Comfort Zones

When we, as twenty-first-century disciples of Christ, break out of our cultural comfort zones and engage with our brothers and sisters of different backgrounds, we will likely be confronted with some striking realities. We will almost certainly hear about life experiences that are very different from our own. A few years ago, I saw an interview that revealed how two people can live in the same land and yet have two totally different experiences of life.

A host on a popular syndicated television show lamented to his African American guest that he was worried that our nation was moving toward a real separation between peoples of different races in our country.

"You think we are *moving toward* one ..." the guest replied. "When did we come together? Were things less intense two hundred years ago? Were they less intense a hundred years ago? In the sixties, were they less intense? In the nineties? You said we are moving toward separation, and that is just not true." The host went on to reiterate that, in his opinion, things seemed to be getting really bad in our nation. The guest responded, "I think things are getting vocalized. I think people who were once marginalized and oppressed now have a voice and are using it. The manner that they are using it, whether on the right or on the left, is a way that offends some."

It seems that in the host's experience, he had never experienced prejudice or discrimination due to the color of his skin. Whatever the case, it is apparent that his experience and awareness were quite different from that of his guest.

For all I know, the host had never experienced feelings of hopelessness due to discrimination. It could be that he had never been racially profiled and followed around in a store. Maybe he had never felt the anxiety of being the only minority in the room or the pain of being denied admission to a club or organization because of the color of his skin. It is possible that he had never experienced the shame and frustration of being pulled over and questioned by law enforcement simply because he was driving in the "wrong" neighborhood. In the end, their conversation made it clear that he had a very different perspective from that of his guest.

Race Is a Learned "Social Construct" ... So Is Empathy

Acclaimed African American Catholic author Toni Morrison once said, "There is no such thing as race. None. There is just a human race—scientifically, anthropologically. Racism is a construct, a social construct ... it has a social function, racism."[16] Just as racism is a learned construct, so is the ability to empathize. To develop empathy, we must seek to develop the skill of "active listening," so we can understand the life experience and feelings of others. This involves knowing how they see the world, which is shaped by their life experiences—especially as they relate to race, ethnicity, and socioeconomic status.

An inability to grasp the historical reality of racism in America was also manifested by a Catholic commentator during St. John Paul II's visit in 1999. In one of his addresses, the Holy Father noted, "As the new millennium approaches, there remains another great challenge facing this community ... [and] the whole country: to put an end to every form of racism, a plague which ... [is] one of the most persistent and destructive evils of the nation." Following the pope's powerful words, this commentator stated that his "curious remarks about racism" demonstrated "how ill-served the Holy Father is by his advisors, since racism is no longer a pressing social issue in the United States."[17]

The Need for Active Listening

The continued prevalence of racial division in the United States is a direct result of not taking the opportunities to listen actively to the experiences of each member in the ethnically diverse body of Christ. Taking the time to hear each other's stories can establish the motivation needed to transform our world into a civilization of love.

As early-twentieth-century American author Alice Duer Miller has said, "People love to talk but hate to listen. Listening is not merely 'not talking,' though even that is beyond most of our powers; it means taking a vigorous, human interest in what is being told to us. You can listen like a blank wall or like a splendid auditorium where every sound comes back fuller and richer."[18]

How do we cultivate the habit of actively listening to the stories of the members of the body of Christ who come from a different racial or ethnic background? The Bible offers some food for thought. In the book of Proverbs, we read, "A fool takes no pleasure in understanding, but only in expressing his opinion" (Proverbs 18:2). I would suggest the practice of "authentic listening" as the starting point for accompanying disciples among different ethnic communities.

When another person is speaking, we sometimes listen only to figure out whether we agree or disagree with what he or she is saying or we are thinking about how we are going to respond. Of course, we will not always agree with what is being expressed. But we should always seek to understand where the person is coming from based on his or her life experiences. For example, a loving parent does not agree with all of the decisions his or her child makes. A loving parent does, however, seek to understand why his or her child made those particular decisions, through the act of listening well.

Listening Well

So how do we listen well? We first need to pray well. St. John Paul II spent hours in prayer every day, and he was universally recognized to be an excellent listener. Why was this the case? Because he was in love with God, and when we are in love, we relish hearing what our beloved has to say. He knew that, since Jesus identified himself with his mystical body—the Church, when people spoke, he was hearing Jesus speaking in and through them.

In the summer of 1980, more than fifty thousand teenagers joined St. John Paul II at Parc de Princes Stadium in Paris. While they came to hear him speak, he was there for a different reason—to listen to them. He said, "I always explain to [young people] that what I tell them is not important. What really matters is what you tell me." At this event, the youth were given the microphone to share their questions. Over the course of three hours, John Paul II listened and responded to each person.[19]

Throughout my life, there have been times when I struggled to understand what God was communicating to me in prayer. When I was in seminary, I tried to wake up every morning and spend an hour with Jesus in Eucharistic Adoration. I distinctly remember sitting in the chapel on some of those days, wondering if I was doing something wrong. I knew God was communicating something to me, but I could not understand what he was communicating.

During this time, I was taking a seminary course taught by two professors who I differed from theologically. Since they were teaching what appeared to be heresy to me, rather than listening to them, I prayed the Rosary or Divine Mercy Chaplet during their class. When I shared this practice with my spiritual director one day, he told me something that radically transformed my life.

"Josh," he said, "I'm disappointed in you. How prideful you are not to listen to your professors just because you don't agree with them. You have admitted that your prayer is very dry right now and that you struggle to perceive what God is saying to you in this season of your life."

He continued his gentle but clear rebuke, "What if God just wants you to sit with him every day in the Adoration chapel because he loves to have intentional time just being in your presence. What if he wants to speak to you later in the day through others, such as your professors, who you don't want to listen to because they think, speak, and act differently than you?"

He reminded me that I knew the voice of God from my time spent with the Scriptures. He encouraged me to listen attentively to the words of my professors, pondering them and then applying them to the Word of God. In this way I would be able to discern what was "of God" and what was not, and receive or reject them accordingly.

So I began to listen with real intention to my professors during class, trying not to judge what they said and determine whether I agreed or disagreed with them. I was to simply listen. The more I pondered what they said—and continued to visit with Jesus each morning in Adoration—the more I heard the voice of God in their lectures. In a short time, I actually began looking forward to hearing what God would say later through the words of my teachers.

The four steps of *lectio divina* can be applied not only to Scripture but also to our interactions with others. As we saw in chapter two, *lectio divina* has four steps: reading, meditation, prayer, and contemplation. After spending time with God, ask him how he is inviting you to respond to a particular conversation or situation so you can receive the spiritual fruit he intends for you to receive. In short, knowing God's voice in prayer helps us to hear his voice in others.

The Holy Pragmatism of St. John de Brébeuf

Many saints were not only holy but wise and pragmatic. One such saint was John de Brébeuf (1593–1649). A Jesuit missionary to the Native American people in what is now upstate New York, St. John lived out the twin ideas of "fasting ... from speaking" and listening well. Trusting in Providence and generous in spirit, he did not reject the native culture where God had placed him but entered into this world so very different from his own.

Like the apostles, St. John de Brébeuf wanted "all nations" to experience the power of Jesus Christ in the sacramental life of the Church. He left the comfort of his home in France and traveled to North America to share the gospel with the indigenous people of the Huron community. To share Jesus with them, he first needed to listen. He listened and learned their language. He listened and learned their history, culture, and spirituality. Once he knew them, he could commune and connect with them. He could then find common ground and invite them to discover how Jesus is the fulfillment of everything they had been practicing.

In time, many Hurons were baptized. Like Jesus and the apostles before him, St. John would be martyred because of his proclamation of the gospel. The indirect fruit of his ministry was the conversion many years later of Kateri Tekakwitha, who would become the first canonized Native American saint. St. Kateri came to know Jesus and the Catholic Church because of the legacy of St. John de Brébeuf—namely, the joy of the gospel he established through intentional listening to and relationship with people very different from him.

Quick to Hear, Slow to Speak

In the New Testament, the letter of James exhorts us to be "quick to hear, slow to speak" (James 1:19). So the fruit of fasting from speaking and intentionally listening to others can truly be supernatural. On the other hand, when we fail to listen well to the stories of all of our brothers and sisters, supernatural fruit will probably not be manifested in our ministries. During the civil rights movement, Dr. Martin Luther King Jr. expressed disillusionment with the Christian ministers in America who did not listen, believe, or seem to care about the suffering Black members of the body of Christ in America. As Dr. King explained to an interviewer,

> The most pervasive mistake I have made was in believing that because our cause was just, we could be sure that the white ministers of the South, once their Christian consciences were challenged, would rise to our aid. I felt that white ministers would take our cause to the white power structures. I ended up, of course, chastened and disillusioned. As our movement unfolded, and direct appeals were made to white ministers, most folded their hands—and some even took stands against us ... My personal disillusionment with the church began when I was thrust into the leadership of the bus protest in Montgomery. I was confident that the white ministers, priests and rabbis of the South would prove strong allies in our just cause. But some became open adversaries, some cautiously shrank from the issue, and others hid behind silence.[20]

One of Dr. King's adversaries was a Catholic bishop. During the march on Selma, Alabama, some Catholics were present, marching alongside Dr. King. The visibility of the Catholic Church is well documented in photographs that circulated in newspapers across the nation. One picture featured twelve priests and four nuns dressed in their clerical and religious attire marching on the front lines for racial justice. Upon seeing priests and nuns at the Selma gathering, the archbishop of Mobile–Birmingham, Thomas Toolen, criticized their participation in the march, saying, "They should be home doing God's work."[21]

Though some Catholic bishops chose not to listen to suffering members of the body of Christ in the Black community, one bishop consistently championed Dr. King's call to action. This bishop was none other than the Bishop of Rome, St. John Paul II. In 1987, the pope visited New Orleans on his pastoral visit to the United States. He spoke of the particular injustices experienced by people of color in America:

> Even in this wealthy nation, committed by its Founding Fathers to the dignity and equality of all persons, the black community suffers a disproportionate share of economic deprivation. Far too many of your young people receive less than an equal opportunity for a quality education and for gainful employment. The Church must continue to join her efforts with the efforts of others who are working to correct all imbalances and disorders of a social nature. Indeed, *the Church can never remain silent in the face of injustice*, wherever it is clearly present ... Today ... we cannot but think of the Reverend Dr. Martin Luther King, Jr., and of the providential role he played in contributing to the rightful human betterment of black Americans and therefore to the improvement of American society itself.[22]

To echo St. John Paul II, it is our mission as a Church to correct that which is disordered in our society. Correcting imbalances cannot be done well apart from listening well and believing those of us who share with you our historical reality, both in America as a whole and in the Catholic Church in particular.

Brothers and Sisters to Us

In 1979, the Catholic bishops of the United States published a pastoral letter on racism entitled "Brothers and Sisters to Us." In this important document, the bishops remind the faithful that racism is a sin that divides the human family, blots out the image of God among specific members of that family, and violates the fundamental human dignity of those who are children of the same Father in heaven. The bishops note that the unhealthy divisions caused by racism are found not just in secular institutions but are also present in the Church.

A few years later, the Black Catholic bishops in the United States collaborated on their own pastoral letter, "What We Have Seen and Heard." They write, "Blacks and other minorities still remain absent from many aspects of Catholic life and are only meagerly represented on the decision-making level ... This racism, at once subtle and masked, still festers within our Church as within our society. It is this racism that in our minds remains the major impediment to evangelization within our community."[23]

Unfortunately, nearly four decades have gone by, and little has changed in Dr. King's accurate assessment that eleven o'clock on Sunday morning is "the most segregated hour in this nation."[24]

We need to see that the racial divisions in this country do not exist solely because people just happen to want to live in the same neighborhoods, go to the same schools, attend the same functions, and worship at the same churches. Many of these divisions are in place because of institutional practices and policies that reinforced the segregation of the past and discrimination based on race. If we, as disciples of Jesus, knowingly and willingly participate in racially prejudiced behaviors or support unjust systems and institutions, then we are not imitating Jesus. We are, in reality, turning our backs on him and the gospel. We are, in fact, imitating the actions of the Evil One.

The struggles of African Americans throughout the history of our nation have been—and continue to be—numerous and varied. Nonetheless, despite the horrific challenges of slavery and racism, Black people have made many beautiful and significant contributions to American culture and society. Let's unpack some of this history as we consider the lives of some heroic people of color.

CHAPTER 5

Black Witnesses in the Body of Christ

On June 17, 2015, a group of twelve Christians gathered together for fellowship, prayer, and study at Mother Emmanuel AME Church. This ecclesial community in Charleston, South Carolina, is a historically Black congregation. As the men and women reflected on the Sacred Scriptures together and shared their hearts with each other, a young man, Dylann Roof, entered the church. He greeted the men and women and asked them if he could join their Bible study. The small group of disciples welcomed him with open arms. Roof participated in the study, asking questions to the pastor and sharing his thoughts as well. Finally, as the Bible study began to wrap up, he vocalized his disagreements with their understanding of the Scripture passages. Instead of debating with him, they graciously listened to his concerns. They invited him to pray with them, and he consented. As they bowed their heads and closed their eyes, Dylann Roof stood up, pulled out his gun, and began to shoot the congregants.

His act of violence ended with the murder of nine out of the twelve members present at the Bible study. Their names were:

Cynthia Hurd, Ethel Lance, Susie Jackson, Reverend DePayne Middleton-Doctor, Reverend Clementa Pinckney Sr., Tywanza Sanders, Reverend Daniel Simmons, Sharonda Coleman-Singleton, and Myra Thompson. All of his victims were Black men and women. Three of his victims survived this domestic terrorist attack. Two of the victims acted like they were dead, and one was left behind to tell the story.[25]

As the story began to make its rounds on the news, Dylann made it clear that he carried out this hate crime because he was a devout racist. Through a jail house manifesto, Roof wrote, "You blacks are killing white people on the streets every day and raping white women every day … I do not regret what I did. I am not sorry. I have not shed a tear for the innocent people I killed."[26] Though it is true that his actions were the result of racist stereotypes and deep-seated racially prejudiced feelings, it is important that we do not limit our understanding of racism to just individual acts of hatred.

Racism is a sin of partiality.* This sin is not just rooted in personal acts of hatred like the massacre Dylann Roof inflicted upon the Mother Emanuel AME Church community. In our nation's history, racism has traditionally been rooted in codified laws and unwritten practices that excluded and discriminated against Black people for no other reason than because of the color of our skin. Legal segregation and direct institutional racism existed in America until the passage of the Civil Rights Acts of 1964. Unfortunately, indirect systems of racism continue to exist in the twenty-first century.

---

* In the New Testament, James warns against the sin of partiality. He writes, "My brethren, show no partiality as you hold the faith of our Lord Jesus Christ, the Lord of glory. For if a man with gold rings and in fine clothing comes into your assembly, and a poor man in shabby clothing also comes in, and you pay attention to the one who wears the fine clothing and say, 'Have a seat here, please,' while you say to the poor man, 'Stand there,' or, 'Sit at my feet,' have you not made distinctions among yourselves, and become judges with evil thoughts? … If you show partiality, you commit sin, and are convicted by the law as transgressors" (James 2:1–5, 9).

Historically, racism against African Americans can be traced directly back to the institution of slavery, which legally existed in America from 1619 to 1865. Ultimately, it took a bloody Civil War, in which more than 600,000 Americans died, and the Thirteenth Amendment to the US Constitution to end slavery. Over the course of nearly 250 years, it is estimated that 10.7 million Africans were abducted, sold into slavery, and shipped to the Americas. An additional two million died during the inhumane voyage from Africa, most from starvation and disease and some from suicide.[27]

Historian John Blassingame describes the horrific travel conditions that led to so many deaths. He notes that slaves had to endure being shackled together naked and forced to lie down in their own blood and human waste, breathing poisonous air while exposed to extreme heat.[28] The slaves who survived the brutal voyage across the Atlantic were forced to labor without pay in the fields owned by their white "masters."[29]

Upon their arrival to America, married African couples were regularly separated from each other and their children, who were sold to different "masters" and plantation owners.[30] Once settled on the plantation, many slaves were beaten or sexually exploited by their masters.[31] Those who resisted were often murdered.

In the Sacred Scriptures, Jesus tells us, "Come to me ... and I will give you rest" (Matthew 11:28). Unfortunately, the slaves who were Catholic weren't even able to find rest in their churches. Catholic monk and historian Fr. Cyprian Davis documented that slaves in St. Martinville, Louisiana, had to ask their owner's permission to receive our Lord Jesus Christ in Holy Communion. Can you imagine? They didn't even have access to Jesus in the Blessed Sacrament unless their master's deemed them worthy. Even still, they were forced to receive our Lord in the Eucharist last in line.[32]

It took nearly two hundred years before a pope condemned the slave trade in America. In the 1839 papal letter ("bull") *Supremo Apostolatus*, Pope Gregory XVI wrote, "We admonish ... all believers in Christ ... that no one hereafter may dare unjustly to molest Indians, Negroes, or other men of this sort; or to spoil them of their goods; or to reduce them to slavery ..."[33]

Despite this clear teaching of the successor of St. Peter, many American bishops, priests, religious, and laity resisted this condemnation of slavery. Perhaps they did not obey the Holy Father because they benefited from this evil institution of slavery or simply believed Black people were inferior. For example, our country's first bishop, John Carroll, owned slaves. Several religious orders built their communities largely on the backs of slaves, including the Jesuits, the Capuchins, the Ursuline sisters, the Carmelites, the Daughters of the Cross, and the Dominican Sisters of Kentucky. The Vincentians in Missouri even owned slaves until the beginning of the Civil War.[34]

Not only did these religious orders commit evil acts against humanity by benefitting from the labor of slaves, but they also denied free men and women of color access to their congregations. One holy woman of African descent, Henriette Delille, who was denied admission to the Carmelites and Ursuline sisters because of the color of her skin, is now on the path to becoming a canonized saint.[35]

The Witness of Henriette Delille

Venerable Henriette Delille was born in 1813 as a free person of color in New Orleans. Since interracial marriage was illegal, her mother, Pouponne Dias, was the concubine of a white man named Jean-Baptiste Delille Sarpy. As an adolescent, Henriette began accompanying Sister Marthe Fontier, a French nun serving in New Orleans. Their mission was to introduce Jesus to free children of color during the day and the Black slaves at night. Together, they tried to form a new, integrated religious community, but it never came to fruition.

Soon, another Frenchwoman, Marie-Jeanne Aliquot, arrived in New Orleans and took over the school for Black children that Sister Marthe began many years earlier. Like Sister Marthe, she also attempted to establish a new integrated religious community to serve the Black community with Henriette, but her efforts failed because such a group would have violated the racial segregation laws of the day.[36]

Henriette continued to work for the salvation of souls as she shared the joy of the gospel with free people of color and Black slaves in her community. Eventually, the vicar general of the Diocese of New Orleans, Fr. Etienne Rousselon, supported her desire to serve and accompany Black people in discipleship in her community. Since joining a white religious order of nuns was not an option for a Black woman, the leadership in the Archdiocese of New Orleans gave her permission to establish a community of Black sisters in New Orleans.

The day she chose to profess her vows as a bride of Christ was symbolic for the order of sisters she was establishing. The date was October 15, 1851, the feast day of St. Teresa of Avila, founder of the Discalced Carmelites. St. Teresa was the granddaughter of a Jewish man who had been forced to convert to Christianity. Teresa experienced discrimination by her fellow Carmelites, as they alienated any sisters whose families were "tainted" with Jewish blood. This discrimination within the Carmelite community was rooted in an official Spanish policy requiring nuns to prove that they were descendants of Christians, not Jews or Moors.[37]

When she established the Discalced Carmelites, St. Teresa of Avila eliminated the "purity of blood" statutes so that women of any ethnicity or bloodline could be admitted into the community. Henriette, a woman who was partially descended from African blood, had been denied access to religious life for several years, so professing her vows on the feast day of St. Teresa of Avila was a powerful statement of racial inclusion in all aspects of the body of Christ.[38]

Her religious profession day turned out to be bittersweet, however. Upon making vows of chastity, poverty, and obedience, most professed religious witness their new identity as brides of Christ to the world by wearing a religious habit and veil. Mother Henriette was denied this opportunity, though, because women of color were not allowed to wear religious habits. So, to distinguish herself from the laity, she wore a black dress and draped a rosary around her neck to identify herself as a religious sister.[39] Her community of sisters would adopt similar attire. It was not until the end of the Civil War, seven years after her death, that the Sisters of the Holy Family were given permission to wear a religious habit with a veil so that they could be formally set apart.[40]

The Witness of the Laity

In addition to the contributions of the Black consecrated women religious, there are countless stories of Black lay men and women who also emptied themselves out for the sake of the gospel. One of these disciples was a woman named Harriet Thompson. In 1853, Thompson, an uneducated Black woman, boldly wrote a letter to Pope Pius IX.

In her letter to the Holy Father, Thompson detailed the hostility of the clergy in her community toward Black Catholics. Not only was her Archbishop indifferent to the evangelization and catechesis of Black men and women, but Black children were being denied access to Catholic schools because their presence would make white children uncomfortable. The children of color in her community were left to attend non-Catholic public schools, where they were being ridiculed for remaining Catholic. Thompson wrote,

> As soon as the teachers find any children in these schools to be Catholics they teach them directly to protest against the church of God. They tell them that the Blessed Eucharist is nothing but a wafer, that the priest drinks the wine himself and gives the bread to us and that the divine institution of confession is only to make money, and that the Roman Pontiff is Antichrists.[41]

Thompson concluded her letter to the Holy Father by writing: "I hope, it is the will of God for the Black race to be saved, something will soon take place for the better."[42] Thompson's words to the Holy Father reveal a disciple of Jesus Christ who loved the Church that our Lord founded but was also not willing to settle with the sinful clergy who participated in the demonic systems of racism. Her letter was so important that the Vatican archived her written words in their Congregation for the Evangelization of Peoples.[43]

Reconstruction and Hope

After centuries of these evils, the bloody Civil War brought slavery to an end. Once the enslaved African Americans were freed following the war and the passage of the Thirteenth Amendment, the nation entered a brief period known as Reconstruction. During this period, federal troops and congressional authorities from the North were sent to the South to enforce the emancipation of the former slaves and ensure that they were being afforded their civil rights and citizenship as American people.[44] Following the horrors of the Civil War, there was hope in the air that good and lasting change would take place between white and Black people, especially in the South but throughout the country as well.

Yet violence against Black people continued.[45] While they were no longer slaves, African Americans faced overt racism and discrimination. As one of the federal soldiers overseeing Reconstruction reported, "Blacks were still forced to stay and work on plantations without any pay. So many freedmen had been killed that the roads and rivers in south Alabama 'stink with the dead bodies' of those who tried to flee."[46]

This hatred was aided by the actions of President Andrew Johnson, who took office following Abraham Lincoln's assassination. For example, while President Abraham Lincoln had signed the Homestead Act of 1862, which granted ownership of land to Black farmers, Johnson oversaw its repeal. As a result, Black farmers never took ownership of land that the federal government had confiscated from former Confederates. This was a dramatic example of how the Black community was taken advantage of through government policy and action.

Despite this racism at the highest levels of government, African Americans began to gain in standing, which led to a certain thriving. The Reconstruction Act of 1867, for example, granted Black men the right to vote for the first time. They quickly began exercising this constitutional right, and in 1872, a Black man, P. B. S. Pinchback, became the first Black governor in the United States. It is interesting to note that he was the last Black man to hold this office until 1990. Although progress was made in the 1800s, much more was still needed.[47]

As African Americans began to gain political power, hard hearts still reigned in whites who could not accept change or see Black citizens as persons equal in the sight of God. Many racial injustices continued to be perpetrated against people of color. As historian Leon F. Litwack writes, "How many Black men and women were beaten, flogged, mutilated, and murdered in the first years of emancipation will never be known."[48]

These sins that were being committed against African Americans would soon become organized, as some former Confederate soldiers founded the Ku Klux Klan.[49] The KKK suppressed the Black vote through violent attacks.[50] More heinously, white mobs successfully lynched at least four hundred African Americans between 1868 and 1871.[51] Between 1877 and 1950, nearly 4,100 lynchings would be reported.[52] Think about this historical fact: an estimated 4,500 Black men and women were hanged in America mainly because of the sins of racial prejudice and discrimination.

Jim Crow and Fr. Augustus

The period of Reconstruction ended in 1877, when the last remaining US Army troops were removed from the South. At this point, the so-called "Jim Crow" laws went into effect. These unjust laws were established to legally segregate white and Black people from each other. People of color were legally excluded from eating, sleeping, residing, walking, riding, working, playing, worshipping, voting, being buried, and doing virtually anything at the same time or place as white people—except working as servants, of course. These laws were based on the principle of "separate but equal," but the accommodations for Black people were always inferior to those used by whites. These laws were enforced by the police, and criminal penalties were given for violating these unjust laws. The laws of segregation would remain in effect until the passage of the Civil Rights Act of 1964, which made such discrimination illegal under federal law

But rays of hope can shine in times of despair. Throughout salvation history, God raises up particular saints to address the specific evils that are present in a particular time and place. For the saints, it was not so much about the specific injustices they faced, but rather who they kept their eyes on—

Jesus himself. Our Church's greatest saints were rooted in their relationship with God through prayer and devotion to the Eucharist. They all knew Jesus, and they turned to him in prayer before they addressed the needs of the people they were sent to serve—and then they went out to preach the gospel of salvation.

During the late 1800s, when Black people in the American South suffered the dehumanizing injustices of the Jim Crow-era laws and prejudices, the Catholic Church in America received its first recognized Black priest, a man named Augustus Tolton.[*] Like others, Fr. Augustus battled against racial prejudice and discrimination, but the fire of love for our Lord burned in him. Fr. Augustus did not allow anything to stop him from answering the Lord's commission to bring the sacraments of the Church and the Word of God to people of every race. Today, he is known as Venerable Augustus Tolton, as his cause progresses toward his canonization as a saint. His example is a beacon for all Catholic leaders today, and his story can inspire us to respond with the same intensity to our Lord's call.

Augustus Tolton was born into slavery in Missouri in 1854. His father escaped and joined the Union Army during the Civil War, ultimately giving his life to end slavery. The same year his father died, Augustus and the rest of his family escaped into the neighboring free state of Illinois.[53] After they arrived, he and his siblings began attending a Catholic school. But all was not well, as they were harassed by the white children, who used racial slurs. Fearing for their safety, Augustus' mother pulled them out of the school. He would begin working in a factory simply to help his family survive. After work, Augustus would meet with a small group of priests

---

[*]   Even though Fr. Augustus Tolton is the first recognized African American priest, the first priest of African descent in the United States of America was James Augustine Healy, who along with his siblings, passed as a white person and thus freely moved through the ranks of society.

and nuns who taught him how to read and write. They also accompanied him in discipleship regarding the ways of the Lord and teachings of the Catholic Church.[54]

One of these priests, Fr. Peter McGirr, saw something special in Augustus, and he strongly encouraged him to receive a Catholic education at the parish school where he served as pastor. He was aware of the backlash that would come from his white parishioners, but he was steadfast in his belief that Augustus deserved to be formed in a Catholic environment. Once Augustus was enrolled, Fr. McGirr began to receive threats. The bishop also received petitions demanding that McGirr be removed as their pastor. The hatred for Black people was so intense in the parish that some parishioners vowed that they would renounce their Catholic Faith if Augustus and his family were not removed from the church and the school.

Despite this persecution, Fr. McGirr persevered in his resolve to stand by Augustus and his family. He was supported by the religious order who taught at the school, the School Sisters of Notre Dame, even when other teachers refused.[55]

Fr. McGirr encouraged Augustus to spend intentional time before the Blessed Sacrament and serve at the altar. When he turned sixteen, Augustus received his First Holy Communion.[56] He would later relate that, while in the presence of our Eucharistic Lord, he perceived a call to the priesthood.

Fr. McGirr supported Augustus' discernment. Augustus applied first to the Franciscans in America, but he was rejected because of his race. His pastor then wrote letters to every seminary in the United States. All rejected Augustus because he was Black.[57]

Augustus was committed to living his faith and witnessing it within the Black community, even while many leaders in the church in America rejected his vocational calling. Over the next few years, Augustus taught Sunday school to Black children, working tirelessly with his mother as they evangelized the wider Black community.

Augustus' bishop encouraged him to be patient until the Josephites, a community of brothers and priests who served African Americans, opened a seminary in Baltimore. While Augustus waited patiently, Fr. Michael Richardt, one of his mentors, wrote a letter on his behalf to the Franciscan community in Rome. In his letter, he detailed the rejection Augustus had received in America simply due to the color of his skin. Finally, this perseverance would bear fruit. In 1880, Augustus was admitted to study at the Urbanum Collegium de Propaganda Fide in Rome.[58] He was welcomed with open arms by the faculty and students there, both as a seminarian and as a human being.

After six years of formation, Fr. Augustus was ordained to the priesthood on Holy Saturday, April 24, 1886, at St. John Lateran Basilica, Rome. His first Mass was celebrated Easter Sunday, 1886, offered in St. Peter's Basilica, Rome. Although he had experienced such dehumanizing treatment, he returned to America with the heart of a missionary. He was intent on forming intentional disciples in the Black community in the Diocese of Alton (now Springfield) in Illinois. Fr. Augustus led his people, both white and Black, through Bible studies, catechism lessons, counseling sessions, and sacramental formation. His Masses were frequently packed to capacity with white and Black parishioners.

Even then, as his ministry bore fruit, Fr. Augustus was persecuted. Instead of rejoicing at his success in bringing the sacraments to all people, some of his white priest brothers took issue with his popularity. One of these priests, Fr. Michael

Weiss, publicly referred to Fr. Tolton as a "nigger priest."[59] He discouraged white Catholics from worshipping with Fr. Tolton and other Black Catholics, and many heeded Fr. Weiss' evil counsel. Among other things, Fr. Weiss even claimed that worshipping with Black Catholics was sacramentally invalid.

Despite this discrimination, as well as the restrictions of the Jim Crow laws, Fr. Augustus worked zealously to fulfill Jesus' Great Commission to "teach all nations." Eventually, his tireless labors would take a toll on his health. In 1897, just eleven years after his ordination, he passed away from heat stroke and uremia.[60] On June 19, 2019, Pope Francis granted him the title "Venerable," as his cause continues to progress toward canonization as a saint.

The fire of love for our Lord burned in Fr. Augustus' soul in a heroic way. Facing injustices and dehumanizing treatment at every turn, Fr. Augustus looked to our Lord for strength. He didn't just know *about* our Lord; he *knew* Jesus and the greatness of his gifts. He heeded the Lord's call to evangelize. Fr. Augustus is a shining example for all Catholics to not allow public disapproval or persecution to prevent us from inviting every person who lives within our geographical boundaries to a relationship with Jesus and his Church.

Yet and still, the barriers faced by Mother Henriette Delille and Father Augustus Tolton in the 1800s would be experienced by countless Black Catholics in the 1900s. Many Black vocations to the priesthood and religious life were discouraged by Catholic leaders, and African Americans who were able to profess vows or be ordained continued to face discrimination and segregation from their white Catholic brothers and sisters.

For example, in 1934, the Divine Word Missionaries were invited by the Bishop of Lafayette, Louisiana, Jules Jeanmard, to serve the Black community there. Four African American priests began to share the joy of Jesus Christ and the Catholic Church with the faithful. These priests, though, were instructed to observe the racial practice of the Lafayette diocese, which included never shaking hands with white priests or attending official functions with the white priests.[61]

Another notable figure during this time was Bishop Harold Raymond Perry. Perry was ordained to the priesthood in 1944. Throughout his priesthood, he was a vocal supporter of the civil rights movement. In the 1960s, due to his prominent role as a leader in the civil rights movement, he was invited by President John F. Kennedy to dialogue with the government about peaceful ways to advance desegregation. A few years after his meeting with the President, he was appointed as auxiliary bishop in the Archdiocese of New Orleans, and his ordination was celebrated by Black Catholics across the nation as he became our first recognized African American bishop.

Unfortunately, large groups of people gathered outside the cathedral on the day of his ordination to protest the event. Some protestors marched with signs that read, "Jesus did not choose non-white apostles," as others shouted, "This is another reason why God will destroy the Vatican."[62]

As racial disunity continued to be perpetuated through the country's laws and practices, some Black and white Catholics worked together with others to abolish the legalized racism then in force. Then, after more than three centuries of injustice, the Civil Rights Act of 1964 was passed. This single law immediately outlawed segregation and discrimination on the basis of race that had been woven throughout our cultural and legal systems. For the first time, people of color had the right to eat, sleep, work, pray, play, vote, be buried, and own property in the same places as whites. Direct institutional racism sanctioned by law was finally eradicated in the United States.

Laws Do Not Change Hearts

The human person is an extraordinary creation. We have been endowed by our Creator with the ability to reason and to choose. Humanity certainly has done amazing things: We have built cathedrals, sacrificed our lives for others in war, and performed acts of service to the poorest of the poor and most vulnerable among us. When God created us, he affirmed our creation by saying, "It is very good." But we would all agree that, through the gift of free will, some of us—many of us—have made some very bad choices. The human heart is also a complex thing. And our hearts can be fickle.

Slavery, reconstruction, and Jim Crow laws are gone. But to this day, less overt—but no less dehumanizing—racist behavior and even racist policies continue to endure in our society. Though they are subtle, there are still places where access to opportunities and accommodations is unequal simply because one is a person of color. Often, these come in the form of vague policies and unspoken practices and are found in places small and large—from remote corners of the internet to the laws that should ensure justice for all. As Pope Francis writes in his encyclical *Fratelli tutti* ("All Brothers"), "Racism is a virus that quickly mutates and, instead of disappearing, goes into hiding, and lurks in waiting."[63]

There continue to be places where exclusion is an unwritten policy. To this day, some social clubs exclude African Americans from membership. These practices are unwritten, so they cannot be traced to any legitimate authority. As a result, many people are unaware of the way these clubs dehumanize Black people. Yet a person of color may be denied membership at a country club under the guise of it being a "private club." Swimming pools, fraternities, sororities, and Mardi Gras balls in Louisiana have remained segregated by color for decades, despite the Civil Rights Act of 1964.

Racial discrimination shows itself not only in being excluded but also in being treated differently on account of one's race. Here is an example. Growing up, I attended a predominantly African American high school. As a priest, I have ministered at predominantly white high schools. So I have experienced firsthand how law enforcement interacts with both student bodies. I can vividly recall law enforcement officers regularly searching my predominantly Black public school for drugs, but I have never witnessed these random searches of students at the predominantly white schools at which I have served.

According to the Department of Health and Human Services, drug use among whites, Blacks, and Hispanics is about equal—6.4 percent of whites, 6.4 percent of Blacks, and 5.3 percent of Hispanics used illegal drugs in the year 2000. In fact, according to research provided by the National Institute on Drug Abuse, "African American twelfth graders have consistently shown lower usage rates than white twelfth graders for most drugs, both licit and illicit."[64] Despite the statistics that show an equal use of drugs between white people and Black people, one group—whites—is typically seen as "experimenting" while the other group—Blacks—is labeled "thugs." Such views and approaches have consequences.

Any person who is convicted of drug charges and goes to prison loses the right to vote in many states—and can be permanently denied access to certain job opportunities or the ability to access ownership in certain neighborhoods.[65] Unequal enforcement of drug laws, then, has serious and damaging consequences for African Americans.

Even drug laws themselves have placed the Black community at a disadvantage. In the 1960s, many people, white and Black people alike, struggled with drug abuse and substance addiction. In 1986, however, the Anti-Drug Abuse Act was passed, which mandated a minimum sentence for distributing cocaine. This law led to much harsher sentencing for crack cocaine, which was predominantly used by people of color and was a cheaper substance, than for powdered cocaine, which was typically used by whites and more expensive.[66] By 1988, the sentences for distribution of illegal drugs had been increased from a maximum of one year in prison to the death penalty in extreme cases.[67]

Many of our laws today continue to disproportionately affect minority communities. Some cities have laws that ban sagging pants due to the possibility of "indecent exposure." Whether intentional or not, the group that this would disproportionately affect is African American teenagers, who invented this fashion style.[68]

Race, Employment, and the Law

While racial inequality in the justice system is deeply disturbing, it is not the only area where African Americans continue to be treated unequally. Despite the many policies and statements that corporations publish assuring equality for all races, a University of Chicago research study revealed a troubling trend.

The University of Chicago sent resumes to companies in response to posted job listings. These resumes were written so that each candidate had similar education and experience, but some had common "white-sounding" names, while others had common "Black-sounding" names.

The researchers discovered that the candidates with more "white-sounding" names received a response after sending ten resumes, while those with traditional "Black-sounding" names needed to send out fifteen resumes before they had any response. This study reveals that bias remains in the business world, setting members in the Black community at an employment disadvantage due to their race.[69]

While great strides have been made to legally protect the rights of minorities in America, laws passed with racial animus in mind continue to exist. On April 20, 2020, in the case *Ramos v. Louisiana*, the Supreme Court overturned a Louisiana law that permitted non-unanimous verdicts in criminal trials. This law dated back to the state's constitutional convention in 1898, and its underlying purpose was to limit the effect African Americans would have on juries. By allowing a verdict of 10–2, for example, a Black person could be convicted of a crime even if only ten of the jurors, who would typically be white, voted to convict.[70] It took more than fifty years after the Civil Rights Act of 1964 for this law to be overturned.

Racism Hits Home

As long as institutionalized racist practices and policies—written or unwritten—continue to exist, people of color will continue to experience discrimination. I speak not just from study of this issue and from the experience of my ministry but from my own personal story. When my parents met in the 1980s, my mother was a registered nurse, and my father was a rising member of the Baton Rouge police department, eventually becoming a captain. My dad grew up in Mississippi and Louisiana under the Jim Crow laws, so he was accustomed to racially prejudiced behaviors and institutional laws that discriminated against African Americans.

My parents fell in love soon after they met. Being a mixed-race couple was not an issue for them, but many in the community would oppose their love and openly attack it. They experienced rejection from co-workers and church members since the time they started dating. They still experience it now in their senior years.

On one occasion, when my parents were out walking together, a random stranger noticed they were holding hands and showed overt disgust at their public display of affection. He actually attempted to walk between them in an effort to keep them apart from each other. My dad was visibly upset. My mom was able to calm my dad down, assuring him that things would get better. Unfortunately, things did not get better. They actually got worse. In time, she too became disillusioned.

In 1985, my parents purchased their first home. When some in the neighborhood learned that an interracial couple was moving in, vandalism of their home followed. Someone even spray-painted a Nazi swastika on my father's police car. The insults continued.

After my mom gave birth to my older brother, Sam, she hired a babysitter to watch him while she worked at the hospital. This arrangement worked well until the babysitter discovered that my brother was biracial. She had assumed he was adopted because he looked Hispanic to her. When she realized that he was the child of a mixed-race couple, she informed my mother that she would no longer watch him.

As my mom's co-workers learned of my parent's interracial marriage, they began to treat her poorly. Some of the white nurses refused to have any relationship with her because she was with a Black man, and some of the Black nurses rejected her because she was with a "good" Black man. Even some of her patients would treat her badly when they learned she was married to a Black man.

If my mom is anything, she is kind. Despite encountering ridicule and rejection, she treats even her persecutors with kindness because she loves the Lord and takes her faith seriously. Her time in prayer enables her to see others as Jesus sees them, with a caring and forgiving heart. Despite rejection by so many due to her marriage to my father, she refused to reject her co-workers and patients—no matter how rude they were to her. She did not want anyone else to experience that pain of rejection. In fact, the more insults she received, the more kindness she gave. Following the spirit of St. Francis, where there was darkness, she brought light, and where there was sadness, she brought joy. This was a powerful and lasting witness to me, even if I frequently fail at living up to her example.

My parents' experiences of racial prejudice continued after they both retired. A few years into my seminary formation, my dad was diagnosed with cancer. During my dad's treatment, my parents went to our neighborhood pharmacy to pick up some prescriptions. As they waited in the parking lot for the prescriptions to be filled, the manager of the pharmacy came out and asked them to leave, or she would call the police. When they asked her why, she told them that another customer had informed her that she had witnessed a Black man getting into a white woman's car. So naturally, she assumed that they must be up to "no good."

After my dad was cancer-free, my mom reconnected with one of her classmates from high school. They spoke every week in anticipation of their forty-year class reunion. This classmate repeatedly told my mom how much she missed her. Imagine my mom's disappointment when, upon arriving at the reunion with my father, her friend treated her coldly because she saw that my mom was married to a Black man. This heartbreaking story shows the pervasive nature of racism, which can negatively affect one's relationships if we let it.

My parents are among the most devout Christians I have ever met. They would certainly be called intentional disciples. Their fidelity to our Lord Jesus, to his Church, and to each other has been tested in fire since their relationship began nearly forty years ago. Yet they have remained steadfast in their fidelity to each other and to God throughout their trials.

Some Personal Experiences

In third grade, an African American classmate told me that Blacks and whites cannot "be together." So I must be adopted, she said. Upset, I went home and asked my mom and dad if they were my biological parents. At this point, they decided it was time to have "the Talk" with me. In the Black community, "the Talk" is when parents uncomfortably inform their children that they will be treated differently by others because of the color of their skin.

In high school, whenever my friends and I went shopping, we would be followed around the store by a security guard. As a high school senior, I remember shopping for my mom one afternoon at the local grocery store. As soon as I walked into the store, a security officer honed in on me and proceeded to follow me down every aisle I walked. After ten minutes of this harassment, I saw no point in giving the store my business, so I left. He then actually followed me out of the store and watched me as I got in my car. He did not go back inside until he saw me drive away. Even today as a priest, if I am wearing "civilian" clothes, I will almost certainly be racially profiled when I go out shopping. Unfortunately, this is not just my experience.

In 2021, Wilton Cardinal Gregory, the first African American cardinal, shared similar words with the *Today* show on NBC. He said, "I don't know any African American who hasn't tasted the bitter cup of discrimination ... Now as long as I am formally dressed, I'm treated with great respect and affection. But if I take off my clerics to go out, to go shopping or run an errand, I'm in the pool of every other African American man in Washington."[71]

Similar to Cardinal Gregory, when I wear my clerical attire in public, even in rapidly secularizing America, I am usually treated with respect. But not always. Every now and then, someone will confront me with a disrespectful racial comment, even though I am a priest. For instance, when I was returning home to the United States from a pilgrimage to Poland, an airport security guard harassed me as I was waiting for my luggage. She actually accused me of not being a "real" priest, suggesting that the clerics I was wearing and my passport picture were fake. While I do not know for sure if the color of my skin was the cause of her accusation, experiences like this are not common amongst my white priest friends.

Then there was also an instance I faced at one of my parish assignments. Soon after I arrived at the Church, a parishioner approached me after Mass and thanked me for all the good work I was doing in the community. The parishioner then leaned in close and whispered, "But you better not bring 'the hood' into our parish."

Jesus Gives Us the Remedy

My own experiences of racial prejudice echo what so many people of color have witnessed and felt over the past four centuries in America, even to this day. I encourage all Catholics to open their minds and hearts to the stories shared by their Black friends and acquaintances. If an African American brother or sister in Christ shares a story with you, intentionally listen and take it to heart. Taking time to listen well to each person in our community is a necessary step in working with people from different backgrounds in our efforts to build a civilization of love.

CHAPTER 6

Reconciling the Body of Christ

One Friday afternoon, on my way to a Catholic high school in Baton Rouge to mentor a senior who was preparing a presentation for his theology class, I met my brothers for lunch at a nearby restaurant.

It was such a gift to be able to spend time with my brothers. Apart from the holidays, we had not shared a meal together since we were kids. After we were seated, we picked up where we had left off the last time we were together. We began by sharing the latest happenings in our lives, then started making fun of each other just like we did when we were kids.

As with most families, my brothers and I carry in our hearts a lifetime of both joyful and painful memories. As lunch went on, we began to disagree about some family issues, and I soon lost custody of my tongue. Before I knew it, I was arguing. Finally, one of my brothers spoke to me bluntly and told me exactly what he thought my faults were.

After lunch, I went to assist the high school student with his project and then drove to a nearby convent to spend some time with Jesus in prayer. I needed to reflect prayerfully on the argument with my brothers, to figure out how our time together had gone wrong. I also needed to examine my heart.

As I spent time with Christ, I suddenly was made aware that God had spoken to me through my older brothers. In the months leading up to that lunch, I had spent hours with Jesus in prayer before the Blessed Sacrament, asking him to reveal to me what vices he wanted me to combat and which virtues he wanted me to cultivate. As is often the case, there was a lot of silence from the Lord.

I have learned that God always speaks to us in his time and manner. We cannot dictate when or how he communicates his mind and will to us in our journey toward eternity. While praying that day in Adoration, it hit me like a ton of bricks— my older brother Matt, by telling me of my faults, did exactly what I had been asking God to do for months. My brother's words were used by the Lord to convict my heart of where I needed to be reformed in my walk with him and his people.

Criticism and Growth in the Lord

I share this story because, no matter how much progress we have made, there is always more room for growth in our relationship with Jesus, the Church, and the world. There is not a day that goes by where I do not recognize my need for deeper purification and personal reformation. This side of heaven, I will fail and continually need to be refined in my walk with Jesus.

He has made me aware of my failures and shortcomings, of the areas in which I need to grow. Our Lord is constantly reforming my heart and renewing my mind. As a pastor, I often encourage my parishioners not to get upset when someone criticizes them, because none of us is perfect—we may actually need to be corrected in our words or behavior. It is important that we do not think too much of ourselves.

One of the saints who knew he was loved by God unconditionally but also that he was not above reproach was St. John Vianney. Early in his tenure as pastor of a parish in Ars, France, some of his parishioners and fellow priests were so fed up with him that they petitioned the bishop for him to be removed from the parish. They claimed he was a lazy priest, an incompetent pastor, and a source of division in the community. Reportedly, St. John Vianney heard about this petition and asked to see it. Upon reading the terrible things that had been written about him, he signed his name to the petition as well! He proclaimed, "They are right!" Ultimately, the bishop, seeing St. John's holiness, let him remain as pastor of Ars. He continued serving his parishioners and spending time with God in prayer.[72]

Like St. John Vianney, we must always be open to being confronted with our "stuff." We must admit that we need God's help and allow him the opportunity to reform us by spending time with Jesus in prayer and frequenting the sacraments, especially Reconciliation.

In a similar way, we need to turn to God for help in righting wrongs in our society and Church. We have spent time in this book reflecting on the wrongs done to the Black community in America, even in the Catholic Church, and the ways that we can reach out to every person who lives within the geographical boundaries of our communities to invite them to the table of the Lord. Here, we come to a supernatural truth that can be hard to understand but is powerful. As disciples of Christ, we need to focus on the deep spiritual wounds that the sins of racism have inflicted on our country and seek to heal them through our acts of repentance, reparation, and reform.

The Church Too Has "Stuff" That Needs Reform

While each of us needs ongoing personal reform and growth, the Church as an institution also needs ongoing reform of its practices and policies. When I first began to serve as pastor, several members of the ministry team shared with me the good and bad of our parish's history. One item was the fact that a number of Catholics from our parish no longer worshipped with us because their children had not been allowed to be confirmed. When I asked why, they told me of the policy that required students to go on a Confirmation retreat and perform a certain number of community service hours, in addition to the prep classes. Any student who missed the retreat, skipped classes, or did not do their service hours would not be allowed to be confirmed.

While I understood the good intent behind these rules—to ensure students were properly prepared to receive the sacrament of Confirmation—I saw that they were not bearing the supernatural fruit for which they were intended. In fact, they had become a barrier to the faith life of the young people and to their reception of the sacrament. Parents and their children were leaving the practice of the sacramental life of the Church. This is the opposite of the goal of sacramental prep, which is to bring people closer to Jesus through these life-giving signs of sanctifying grace.

The situation prompted me to look at the Code of Canon Law to see what legitimate restrictions there were or options that could be used. I learned that no canon mandates that a student preparing for Confirmation need to attend a certain amount of classes, participate in a retreat, and fulfill service hours. It simply requires that a person know what the sacrament of Confirmation is and that he or she desires to receive the gifts of the Holy Spirit. So, to better accommodate the youth in our community, my team and I rewrote the policy to encourage students to attend the classes, participate in the retreats, and do service hours but did not require them to do so. This does not mean, however, that we went "soft" on their formation. On the contrary, our plan often involved personally meeting with the candidates one-on-one for instruction.

The lesson we learned is that our impulse in faith formation should be to stretch our capacity for the sake of meeting people where they are within the bounds of our abilities and resources. I believe that if we have the will, the Lord will help us find a way.

Overall, as a team of disciples, we need to discern if our ministries are bearing supernatural fruit or if we are unintentionally pushing people away from Christ and his Church. Policies and procedures are usually composed by good people with good intentions, but they are not infallible. It is important that we continually re-examine our approaches to see how we might improve them. To do this, we need to listen, learn, pray, and go back to the table to reform them for the good of those we serve.

Taking a Fresh Approach

This approach doesn't apply just to our parishes and the Church as a whole. It can also be applied to every sector of our society. Over the years, I have been fortunate to consult with the district attorney, and through our collaboration, I am well aware of how many good men and women serve our communities in the police department, placing themselves in dangerous situations for our safety. Even before I worked with law enforcement in my present role, I was aware of the dangers police officers face because I grew up as the son of a police captain. While dressed in uniform, my father was shot at multiple times, including point-blank in the back of his head. As a child, I vividly remember staying up all night wondering if my father would make it home or if he had lost his life while protecting and serving the people of our community.

He was a virtuous cop, but that doesn't mean he was perfect; like all of us, he had areas in which he needed to grow, where he needed reform. Likewise, my father will testify how he witnessed significant change, progress, and reform in the police department during his many years on the job.

In his early years as a police officer, he was not permitted to arrest white people. This was an unwritten rule, but it was vigorously enforced by the police department. Later in his career, though, he would become the first African American officer to arrest a white man in Baton Rouge. Because he was Black, however, and the offender was white, the case was thrown out of court. Thankfully, this type of overtly racist approach no longer happens, and this is an example of the positive reform that has taken place in our criminal justice system. While these types of situations were more prevalent thirty or more years ago, there are still incidents of racial bias among law enforcement that reveal continued reform is needed.

Early in his days on the police force, my father worked alongside men who he knew were members of the KKK. They were dangerous, not so much because of the white robe they wore at night but the badge they wore during the day. Instead of protecting and serving their community, these men instilled fear in the minds of African Americans in Baton Rouge as they harassed them for no reason other than because of the color of their skin.

One night, my father and his partner were patrolling the streets. While pulled over in a parking lot, they watched from their vehicle as another patrol car pulled up beside a young Black man. Four white officers exited the car, and without warning or warrant, began to jump on this man, beating him with their fists, boots, and batons. My father and his partner immediately rushed to stop the assault. The four white officers tried to lie to my father about what had happened, but he and his partner had witnessed the entire scene. Against my dad's protest, they arrested the young man. In court, my father argued in the young man's defense, and he was released without being charged. The four officers who beat him, though, were never held accountable.

As my father rose in the ranks of the Baton Rouge Police Department, he saw much change in the hearts and minds of his fellow cops. He also saw unjust practices and policies change for the better. Still, there remains room for more improvement. The department is made up of imperfect human beings, so there will always be a need for continued reform and improvement in the individuals and in the institution's written rules and unwritten practices.

Reform and Reparation

Reform is a well-known concept to Catholics—both as individuals seeking to grow in our relationship with Jesus and as a Church community. Throughout its history, the Church has examined herself and made significant reforms. For example, after the scandal of the clergy sexual abuse came to the light in the early 2000s, new policies were established to protect our youth and vulnerable adults from sexual predators. Among other things, the requirements for men applying to the seminary became more rigorous. Ongoing background checks and safe environment workshops have become mandatory for any minister volunteering for or working in the Church.

Bishops who allowed pedophile priests to be moved from parish to parish have been held accountable. Now, any priest who has a credible accusation against him is removed from ministry, and the accusation is shared with law enforcement and the general public. These reforms have helped reestablish trust in those who have been hurt by the actions of priests and Church leaders in the past. I propose that similar reforms can help people of color in the body of Christ reestablish trust with their white brothers and sisters in the Lord.

An essential component of reformation is reparation. The term is commonly understood to mean financial reparations, and while I agree that we should study economic restitution, which is what Georgetown University has been addressing over the past few years,* the purpose of this section is to address the biblical concept of reparation: the act of making things "right" between us and God—and with each other.

An example of reparation in the New Testament is the encounter between Jesus and the tax collector Zacchaeus. As Jesus was passing through Jericho, Zacchaeus wanted to see him but could not get a glimpse of Jesus due to the crowds. So he climbed up into a tree to get a clearer view. At that point, things get interesting:

> When Jesus came to the place, he looked up and said
> to him, "Zacchaeus, make haste and come down; for
> I must stay at your house today." So he made haste
> and came down, and received him joyfully. And when
> they saw it they all murmured, "He has gone in to be
> the guest of a man who is a sinner." And Zacchaeus
> stood and said to the Lord, "Behold, Lord, the half of

---

*   In the nineteenth century, Georgetown University, a prominent Catholic institution of higher learning, owned slaves and sold 272 of these men, women, and children to Southern plantations for an amount equivalent to 3.3 million dollars today. To make restitution for their participation in the sin of slavery, Georgetown is raising $400,000 a year to benefit the descendants of the slaves who were separated from their families and sold to keep the college afloat.

> my goods I give to the poor; and if I have defrauded
> any one of anything, I restore it fourfold." And Jesus
> said to him, "Today salvation has come to this house,
> since he also is a son of Abraham. For the Son of man
> came to seek and to save the lost." (Luke 19:5-10)

Here is some background. In biblical times, tax collectors
were seen as public sinners in the community because they
could legally take disproportionate sums of money from the
Jewish citizens of their town. Zacchaeus was seen as the
most troubling of Jericho's tax collectors. For Jesus to enter
his house and stay with him would have scandalized the
community, but it transformed Zacchaeus' heart. He could
not believe that Jesus wanted to be in a relationship with him
after all he had done. His heart was moved to repentance. He
said, "Behold, Lord, the half of my goods I give to the poor."

Zacchaeus not only repented of his sins to Jesus, but he also
desired to be reconciled with the people in his community.
Reconciliation is needed to reestablish trust, which is not
established simply by apologizing to the person wronged.
Trust is built only when the sinner repairs the wrong he or
she has done.

I can attest to this with a personal anecdote. As a seminarian,
I went on a retreat with a priest friend. Since his car was in
the shop, he borrowed his mother's vehicle. It was 2011,
and I had not yet driven a car with a rear-facing "back up"
camera. After the retreat ended, we made our way to the
parking lot. Since he had driven us to the retreat, I offered to
drive us home. As I put the car in reverse, I got distracted by
the little screen on the dashboard that showed me backing
up. As I got closer to the other vehicles, I heard a "beeping"
noise. Distracted, I took my eyes off of the screen to find
out where the noise was coming from, and I crashed into a
parked car!

What a way to end our retreat! I felt terrible. We waited for the owner of the vehicle to arrive so I could apologize and exchange insurance information. Upon discovering that I was a seminarian, the man generously offered to take care of his car himself. I was grateful. But there was more that still needed to be done. I still had to apologize to my friend's mom for damaging her car.

Generous in spirit, this Christian woman forgave me immediately. Even still, we were not reconciled yet. I still had to make things right and repair the damage I had done to her car. In other words, I needed to make reparation for mutual trust between us to be established.

Likewise, Zacchaeus apologized for his years of taking advantage of the people in his community. But he was not reconciled with his neighbors until he made an act of reparation. He generously returned what he had stolen four times over. As a Jew being restored to his community, he paid back what he had taken fourfold because it was the law.

In the book of Exodus, we read about the reparation that was legally expected of a person who stole from another: "If a man steals an ox or a sheep, and kills it or sells it, he shall pay five oxen for an ox, and four sheep for a sheep. He shall make restitution" (Exodus 22:1). Similarly, in the book of Numbers, we read, "He shall confess his sin which he has committed; and he shall make full restitution for his wrong, adding a fifth to it, and giving it to him to whom he did the wrong" (Numbers 5:7).

The following words might be difficult to read—and require nuance in how they are expressed and understood. Because slavery was a sin committed by our nation, every generation of Americans needs to do penance for this sin and make reparation for it. Here, I am speaking of a spiritual reparation.

As disciples of Christ, we need to focus on the deep spiritual wound slavery has inflicted on our country and seek to heal it through our acts of repentance and reparation.

A natural reaction to this statement, though, might be: "Why do I have to do penance and offer reparation for something in which I did not participate? No one in my family owned slaves! I have never uttered a racial slur or discriminated against others because of their race! I never participated in an institution that promoted racist practices and policies!"

Repentance and Reparation in the Bible

The Bible offers us the reason why we are all responsible for making reparations to bring about reconciliation in our nation. In Scripture, the Greek word for repentance, *metanoia*, means both "turning away" from sin and toward God as well as doing penance for our transgressions. When Jesus tells those who would be his followers to "repent, and believe in the gospel" (Mark 1:14), he was inviting them to turn away from any sinful ways and do penance for their past offenses.

In the Old Testament, the prophet Ezra offered up prayers and penances, not only for his personal sins, but also on behalf of the transgressions of the community.

> And at the evening sacrifice I rose from my fasting, with my garments and my mantle torn, and fell upon my knees and spread out my hands to the LORD my God saying: "O my God, I am ashamed and blush to lift my face to you, my God, for our iniquities have risen higher than our heads, and our guilt has mounted up to the heavens. From the days of our fathers to this day we have been in great guilt; and for our iniquities we, our kings, and our priests have been given into the hand of the kings and our priests have been given into the hand of the kings of the lands, to the sword, to captivity, to plundering, and to utter shame, as at this day." (Ezra 9:5-7)

In a similar way, the prophet Daniel prayed to the Lord about his sins, those of his people, and their ancestors: "To us, O Lord, belongs confusion of face, to our kings, to our princes, and to our fathers, because we have sinned against you" (Daniel 9:8). He took on the responsibility of praying on behalf of his entire community so that they might be reconciled with God.

Likewise, in the New Testament, St. Paul exhorts the Christians in Corinth, "If one member suffers, all suffer together" (1 Corinthians 12:26). The Catholic Church in America has members who are suffering from racist practices and policies, as well as from the effects of generational racism. We also have members of our Catholic family lineage who enslaved, persecuted, and oppressed African Americans for years and never repented. As a Church, we are called to offer prayers for the people whom Catholics have persecuted and for those who are in purgatory because of their participation in racial injustices. In addition to offering prayers, we are called to do penance on their behalf as well.

Jesus never committed any sins, but he took on the sins of others. St. Paul invites the Colossians, and all Christians, to join Jesus in offering up their sacrifices and sufferings for the good of the Church: "Now I rejoice in my sufferings for your sake, and in my flesh I complete what is lacking in Christ's afflictions for the sake of his body, that is, the Church" (Colossians 1:24). Here, Paul is not suggesting that there is anything "lacking" or insufficient in Jesus' suffering, death, and resurrection. One drop of Christ's blood is sufficient to save the entire world. But St. Paul was saying that his sufferings are a vehicle God used to convey the sufferings of Jesus to the hearts and souls of men and women.[73] St. Paul took on Christ's suffering in himself and offered them on *behalf* of others.

This is what many priests, including myself, have done since the revelations of widespread clergy sexual abuse came to the light. I have never abused or wanted to abuse another person. However, because I am a priest, I have taken on penances specifically for the healing of people in my community who have been abused by priests. As I preached against bishops who tolerated and enabled these priests, I also prayed for the healing of those who had been affected by their sins. I have fasted and performed acts of penance to make reparation for their sins. In addition to taking on penances and offering up reparation for that particular sin, any time a person comes to celebrate the sacrament of Reconciliation, I not only give them a penance, but I also offer up sacrifices for them. This is something every priest is called to do for those who come to receive God's mercy in this powerful sacrament. Though we did not commit their sins, we are responsible for offering penance with them and for them because we are all connected in the body of Christ.

No sin is done in isolation. Every sin we commit has a ripple effect and inflicts a wound on others and on our community. Our nation is still bearing the effects of the country's original sin of codified racism against people made in the image of God. Even if these transgressions were committed by others, all of us are dealing with the effects of these grievous sins on our nation—and each of us can contribute to making reparation for them. We can help bring healing to our nation and our Church, one intentional act at a time.

Truthfully, anything you can do to heal this particular wound in the history of our Church and nation is a noble act, worthy of a modern disciple of Jesus. So how can you offer up the reparations needed for authentic reconciliation and heal racial division in the body of Christ?

Here are six suggestions:

- Encourage your pastor or another priest to offer Masses of reparation.

- Do holy hours of reparation before the Blessed Sacrament.

- Recite the Liturgy of the Hours, with reparation as a specific intention.

- Pray the Rosary or the Divine Mercy Chaplet.

- Pray the Stations of the Cross for racial reconciliation and unity.

- Fast or perform some acts of penance for this intention.

Reparations are the responsibility of the body of Christ, the Church. Jesus desires for all of his people to come together as one, reconciled with each other at the table of the Eucharist. Authentic reconciliation happens when disciples of Christ not only work together for individual and communal reformation, but also pray and fast together through actions of reparation. I believe the Lord will hear your intentional prayers, both for present-day challenges and the sins of the past, and accept your offering.

CHAPTER 7

Representing the Body of Christ

A few years after my ordination to the priesthood, I took a road trip with my parents to Alabama for a weeklong retreat. We celebrated Mass together every day and spent time with Jesus in the Blessed Sacrament. We also visited some Catholic holy sites in the surrounding area, including a gift shop at one. This is when things took an unexpectedly ugly turn.

Most Catholics are familiar with the image of St. Michael the Archangel in which he is stepping on the head of the serpent. The gift shop at this pilgrimage site had several statues of St. Michael. One depicted him as a white man with blond hair and blue eyes with his foot on the devil, pushing him down. The problem is that the devil was portrayed as a brown-skinned man with features that might be identified as African American. Although likely unintentional, the end result was a white man with his foot on the head of a brown-skinned man.

I had entered the gift shop ahead of my parents, and I prayed that they would not notice this statue. I knew it would offend them as much as it was offending me. With some effort, I attempted to steer them away from the statue, which clearly brought sadness to my heart. Unfortunately, my father's eyes spotted it.

He pulled me aside and asked, "Son, did you see that?" I said, "Yeah, Dad." He said, "That's just not right, son. That's just not right."

I then approached the woman at the checkout desk and asked her to remove the statue, or at least have it repainted. She told me she knew the artist who created it and that he did not intend it to be racially offensive. Therefore, she would not have it removed or repainted. I told her that my father was not Catholic, and statues like this are barriers for him and many others from becoming Catholic. She was unmoved.

The Power of Images

Paintings, statues, mosaics, icons, and stained glass windows can be gifts that draw people to a relationship with Jesus Christ and the sacramental life of the Church—if they accurately reflect the teachings of the gospel. If not, they can be barriers for people who are being drawn to the Catholic Church.

I know this all too well from personal experience. My older brother, like me, drifted away from active participation in the Church as a teenager. A few months after my ordination, he reached out to see if I could help him grow in his relationship with Jesus. After being away from Christ in the sacraments for a number of years, he recognized a void in his life. My heart was filled with joy because I had prayed and fasted for years for my brothers to come back to Jesus through the sacramental life of the Church.

Since the timing worked out, I was able to get my brother signed up for an upcoming silent retreat. After attending this retreat, he was eager to go back to Mass. I have no idea what stirrings the Holy Spirit worked in his heart during those three days of silence, but he was now on fire for Jesus! On his way home from the retreat, he went to a nearby parish and spent a few moments in prayer, thanking the Lord for the life-changing retreat. He then attended Mass, at which the celebrant gave a dynamic homily. My brother was excited to be back home in the Catholic Church. That is, until he noticed a statue in the church of St. Michael that resembled the one that had offended my father and me in the gift shop.

As he looked around at the rest of the congregation, he noticed that he was the only Black person present. Repulsed at the statue's image of the devil as a Black man, my brother left upset and called me to express his anger at what he had seen. In his mind, statues like that reinforced the narrative he heard often from his friends—that the Church was a racist institution. I assured my brother that the pastor of the parish was probably unaware of how offensive and hurtful that particular statue was to African Americans and that he did not place it there to reinforce racist attitudes among his parishioners. Nonetheless, the damage had been done.

Making an Impact

What may seem insignificant to some believers may have a lasting impact on others. This was certainly the case at one of our diocesan high schools. During Black History Month a few years ago, a history teacher invited his students to write a paper on the contributions that African Americans have made to American society. Instead, one of his seniors wrote about her disdain for Black people in America.

In her paper, she wrote that Black people ruined everything, were an embarrassment to this country, and were not represented in the apostles that Jesus chose, who were clearly white men according to her understanding. The student shared her paper with a classmate, and soon it went viral on social media and the local news. The hurt and pain this paper caused throughout the school and the community was substantial—and had the capacity to be extremely divisive. The principal took swift action. Among other things, she asked me to help her and the school faculty respond to the racial division that was created among the student body due to this student's paper.

Before meeting with the faculty, I spent an hour in the school's chapel praying to Jesus in the Eucharist so that I could clearly communicate what he wanted me to say. As I knelt, I noticed some images and statues of Jesus, Mary, Joseph, and St. Michael the Archangel—all of whom were depicted as white. Yet again, the only person depicted with black skin was Satan under the foot of St. Michael.

Reflecting on the student's paper, I wondered if she assumed that biblical figures were white because that was the only visual representation of them she saw in the school chapel, and perhaps her home parish. As I walked through the hallways to the classroom where I was to give my presentation, I noticed more images of saints—and they too were white. Knowing the cultural and racial diversity of this Catholic school, I wondered why the images of holy persons on its walls did not represent the diverse members of the body of Christ in the kingdom of heaven.

As I began my presentation, I shared my observations with the faculty. Many were open about being completely unaware of this reality and its possible impact on the students' frame of reference.

I invited them to participate in the narrative Bishop Braxton included in his letter "The Racial Divide in the United States," which imagines a Catholic Church in the United States where people of color are the majority of its members.

I encourage you to read all that Bishop Braxton wrote below as it unpacks, through story, key insights into the often-difficult experience of being Black and Catholic.

> Imagine yourself as a white American teenager living in a poor urban area with few opportunities for you to get a good education and find meaningful employment. Imagine that some of your friends are troublemakers and when the African American police come around they often intimidate them. This frightens you because another white friend of yours was shot and killed by African American police when he reached into his pocket for his wallet which they thought was a gun. Since you were very young, your parents have cautioned you to avoid contact with the police because they may suspect you of wrongdoing.

> You and your friends, whose families are struggling to make ends meet, live near the neighborhood Catholic Church. You have never been inside the church. You and your family are not members of the Catholic Church ... Now imagine that an African American acquaintance, sensing that you are discouraged, persuades you to go with him to this very church, St. Charles Lwanga, for Mass. You enter the church and all images of the sacred are in Afrocentric art. All images of Jesus, Mary, Joseph and all the saints are as People of Color (African, Hispanic, Asian, or Native American). God the Father Himself is painted on the ceiling of the church as a distinguished older black gentleman. You think to yourself, "God the Father is absolute spirit. He has no race or nationality, or anatomical gender. Scripture never describes him as an elderly, African-looking, brown skinned man." You wonder if the Catholic Church believes that only people of African ancestry are in heaven.

> You notice that even the angels in the church have African features. If angels have no bodies and no

gender, if they are pure spirits, why are they not represented in all races? Just think of the impact it would have on un-churched white people, like you, if they encountered the image of a magnificent white angel with blond hair and blue eyes when they entered a Catholic Church. You also notice that in the Catholic Church "black" symbolizes everything that is "good" and "holy" whereas "white" symbolizes evil and sin. The images of Satan, the devil, and demons in the church are all white. Later, you search art books and cannot find one image of Satan painted in dark hues. He is always depicted in light, pale colors.

You ask your African-American acquaintance, "Wouldn't the Catholic Church be more truly universal and welcoming of all if the holy men and women of the Bible were pictured as people of different ethnic and racial backgrounds? After all, though we know they were Jewish, no one knows what they actually looked like. All Semitic people do not look like western Europeans." He responds, "That question has been asked before and the response has usually been people who are white should realize that the Afro-centric art represents them as well. Afro-centric art is universal. The all-Black religious art is there for historical reasons. Even though a few churches have added a white saint here and there, for the most part the few white Catholics we have in the church have simply accepted the fact that the majority of churches have few or no images of the citizens of Heaven who look like them."

You ask your acquaintance, "Does the Catholic Church intend to perpetuate this all-Black image of heaven in the churches of the future?"

Your African American acquaintance replies, "There are a few churches in big cities with a large number of 'minorities' where they have painted white angels and saints. But some of the older white people don't like it. They say they do not believe God looks like them. In many countries where all of the people are

European, the people almost never complain about the all-African religious art."

"But," you ask, "what about here in the racially diverse United States? What a powerful statement the Church would make if she mandated all future churches to have racially diverse images of God, Jesus, Mary, saints, and angels? Wouldn't it convey a more authentically universal image of heaven?"

He answers, "I really don't think that is ever going to happen."

"Why not?" you ask. "Why not?"[74]

Since the faculty and administration of this high school were exclusively white, it was possible that they never noticed how the all-white images of holiness in the chapel could have negatively affected the entire student body.

I encouraged the faculty to incorporate more diverse images of holiness throughout the school to show all of the students they all had the capacity to become saints. Within weeks of my presentation, the school's campus minister, in collaboration with the principal, incorporated diverse images of Marian apparitions throughout the campus.

Depicting the Universal Church

Historically, Jesus and Mary were Jews who were born and raised in the desert of the Middle East. They certainly did not look like northern Europeans of today; they would not have had white skin or blond hair and blue eyes. As Jews of Palestine, they would have been of dark complexion, much like the people native to that region today.

After his resurrection, however, Jesus appeared to his disciples in his glorified body. In his glorified body, Jesus no longer looked like he did in his earthly life. In multiple instances, when Jesus appeared to the disciples after his resurrection, they did not recognize him. For example, when he appeared to Mary Magdalene at the tomb on Easter Sunday, she mistook him for the gardener (see John 20:15). It was not until he said her name that Mary Magdalene recognized Jesus in his glorified body. Similarly, the disciples on the road to Emmaus did not know the man who was accompanying them was Jesus until the "breaking of the bread" (see Luke 24:13-35).

Jesus looked different after his resurrection because he was walking and talking in his glorified condition. In the *Summa Theologica*, St. Thomas Aquinas cites the teachings of St. Gregory, who asserted that the resurrected body of Jesus was of the same nature but of a different glory.[75] In his glorified body, Jesus vanished from sight (see Luke 24:31), appeared in different forms (see Mark 16:12), walked through locked doors (see John 20:19), and ascended into heaven (see Acts 1:9).

Since his first appearance to Mary Magdalene after the Resurrection, Jesus has continued to appear to his disciples over the past two thousand years—and the Blessed Virgin Mary has appeared to his followers throughout the centuries in all parts of the world. Typically, when Jesus and Mary appear, their image changes to resemble the people to whom they are appearing. For instance, when Jesus appeared to St. Faustina in Poland in the twentieth century, he looked European to her. When Mary appeared in Guadalupe, Mexico, in the sixteenth century, she looked like an indigenous Mexican. More than five hundred years after her apparition in Mexico, she appeared as an African woman in Kibeho. So it is entirely appropriate to have ethnically diverse images of Jesus and Mary, as they appear in glory.

In my presentation to the high school faculty, I also pointed out the way they recited prayers over the intercom throughout the day. I asked if any of the prayers specifically addressed the current racial tension in the school. Were they intentionally praying for racial unity among the students? They admitted that they were not. In response, I shared with them a recent prayer the bishop requested that our diocese recite for racial harmony and encouraged them to incorporate it in their school rotation. Within a week, they were reciting a prayer for racial harmony every Friday.

Here is an example of such a prayer:

God our Father, you call us to love one another as you have loved us. We pray for the conversion of hearts and the renewal of minds in our nation. We desire to console the heart of Jesus by cultivating racial healing and reconciliation in the Church.

Through the power of the Holy Spirit, strip us of our pride, mistrust, and prejudices, so that we may be able to listen well, dialogue with one another, and repent for our sins and the sins of other members of the body of Christ.

Lead us to work together to reform unjust practices and policies that continue to perpetuate the racial divide in our society.

We ask these blessings trusting in the infinite mercy of Jesus and the intercession of Mary our Mother. Amen.

Mother Henriette Delille, pray for us. Fr. Augustus Tolton, pray for us. Mother Mary Lange, pray for us. Pierre Toussaint, pray for us. Sister Thea Bowman, pray for us. Julia Greely, pray for us.

Finally, I invited the principal to check the policies in the student handbook for any policies that might be accommodating the white students while discriminating against the Black students. When examined closely, certain policies that at first appear benign and neutral can actually be more challenging for one group than another.

For example, most workplaces and schools have policies regarding hairstyles to discourage overly flamboyant or distracting self-expression. Some of these policies, however, are written in such a way that the only permitted hairstyles are of mainstream American or European culture—that is, they are common among whites. For instance, many Black women have hair that will not naturally straighten unless they perm it. For these Black women who choose not to perm their hair, their styling choices are limited. They can allow their hair to grow naturally into an "Afro" hairstyle, or they can braid it in a number of ways. The problem is that many workplaces and schools have policies that deem these hairstyles inappropriate.

Following conversations with some of the Black students and their parents, the principal became aware that the current hair policy of the student handbook unintentionally discriminated against African American hair. The policy, in effect, reprimanded students from braiding their hair. Many of the Black girls did not feel welcome at the school because they had two choices: perm their hair to look more "white" or grow an Afro. Because the principal did not personally have to face this dilemma, it didn't dawn on her that this was a problem. Nor did she consider that some of the handbook's policies might be racially biased. The principal immediately revoked the hair policy, and she invited the African American students and their parents to help her rewrite the handbook to eliminate any other unintentional discrimination in its written rules.

Servant of God Sister Thea Bowman addressed the importance of representation at the leadership tables in our Church when she spoke to the Bishops of the United States in 1989. She said,

> You know, Bishop Jim Lyke said a long time ago that black Catholic Christians will be second-class citizens of the church until they take their places in leadership beside their brothers and sisters of whatever race or

national origin ... The majority of priests, religious and lay ministers who serve the black community in the United States still are not from the black community, and many of those people who attempt to serve among us do not feel an obligation to learn or understand black history or spirituality or culture or life, black tradition or ritual ... I travel all over the country, and I see it: black people within the church, black priests, sometimes even black bishops, who are invisible. And when I say that, I mean they are not consulted. They are not included. Sometimes decisions are made that affect the black community for generations, and they are made in rooms by white people behind closed doors.[76]

When people of color are represented at the policy-making level, rules that are more just and inclusive can be implemented. If such policies are just, then they are more likely to be a bridge for people to abide together in the sacraments rather than a barrier.

Images in Our Churches

As I have mentioned, I was assigned as pastor of Our Lady of the Holy Rosary Church in St. Amant, Louisiana, in 2017. After looking at the church, I felt called to add a "wall of saints." I wanted the wall to include images of diverse saints so that everyone who came into the church would see someone who looked like them or had a similar story—saints of African descent such as Sister Josephine Bakhita, Friar Martin de Porres, and Charles Lwanga; Native American saint Kateri Tekakwitha; and Mexican saints Fr. Miguel Pro and Juan Diego. I also included saints of European background such as Bernadette of Lourdes, John Paul II, and John XXIII. This wall includes men and women who were married, single, clergy, and religious. There are children and elderly individuals depicted as well. It is important that, if at all possible, everyone who comes to worship at our parish leaves knowing that someone who looks like them or who has a similar story can provide inspiration for them on their walk toward eternity—and encourage them to become a saint!

After the church's wall of saints was complete, we began adding images of saints in our community center. Each of the rooms in the cafe has a Scripture verse on the wall and an image of a diverse saint who is interceding for the people in that space. The association with specific saints, in each room, was so that our patrons (whom we call "clients") and visitors would see someone who looked like them or had a similar story. The images include those of the third-century African martyrs, Perpetua and Felicity; the visionaries of Fatima, Francesco, Lucia, and Jacinta; and the French patron of the poor, Vincent de Paul. In addition to these and many others, we portrayed diverse images of the Blessed Virgin Mary, including Our Lady of Kibeho, Africa; Our Lady of Guadalupe, South America; and Our Lady of the Holy Rosary, Europe.

In addition to our churches and schools, we also should examine our other diocesan institutions. In the spring of 2016, civil unrest started in Baton Rouge after the shooting of a Black man named Alton Sterling. Since I was working closely with my bishop, Robert Muench, on the issue of racial harmony in my diocese, I shared with him my concerns regarding a prominent piece of artwork displayed in our diocesan offices. It was a historical image of a slave-owning Catholic priest as he blessed a rebel flag after the Civil War and was being arrested by the troops from the Union.

As a seminarian, I recall being greatly disturbed when I first saw this painting. I knew that many Black people who had visited the chancery were also offended. Eventually, it was removed and placed in the diocesan archives. About a year after its removal, our diocese's Racial Harmony Commission and Office of Black Catholics were invited by our new bishop, Michael Duca, to frame a new image that better reflected the universality of the Church. It was of the Black Madonna with the Child Jesus, surrounded by six Black Catholics on the path to becoming canonized saints: Mother Henriette Delille, Mother Mary Lange, Fr. Augustus Tolten, Pierre Toussant, Julia Greely, and Sister Thea Bowman.

As director of vocations for the Diocese of Baton Rouge, I have an office in the chancery. As a result, I have witnessed firsthand a number of Black people stand in awe of these images of the African Americans on the path to being canonized saints and the Black Madonna with the child Jesus—holy ancestors who look like them physically. It is my hope that the inspiration of these holy Black men and women will motivate people of color to imitate their virtues and one day join them in the kingdom of heaven.

Witness on the Walls to the Witness of Words

While images on the walls are powerful, the living witness of people today can be even more powerful. For many people of color, it is very meaningful when we see ourselves represented in the leadership of the Church.

I remember when I was first discerning the priesthood, I had a certain doubt about my vocation because I had never seen a Black priest, among other reasons. Shortly before I was ordained, my former pastor put my picture in his parish bulletin and encouraged his parishioners to pray for me as I prepared for my ordination. A young African American boy saw my picture and was shocked that a Black person was becoming a priest. He said to his mother, "Mama, I didn't know we could be priests too!" Unfortunately, this view is held by many Black

Catholic young men—and it has undoubtedly had a negative impact on the number of vocations among African Americans.

Seeing people of color represented in the priesthood, diaconate, and religious life can inspire young people to discern if they too are being called to this vocation. Similarly, when the parish holds an event, it can be particularly helpful for conference or retreat participants to hear the message of Jesus from someone who looks like them. Even inviting parishioners of color who are the regular Mass-goers to become lectors, ushers, greeters, and altar servers will have a positive effect on the entire parish.

The Message Must Speak to Everyone

One of my colleagues in the chancery, Dina, has been intentional in ensuring that our diocesan events have diverse speakers who represent all of the people of our diocese. She has a sincere desire to become a saint, and to form saints across cultural lines throughout the community. As the director of evangelization and catechesis, she often collaborates with Catholic leaders throughout the country to schedule evangelization and discipleship conferences, spiritual retreats, and workshops on catechesis throughout the year.

In one instance, Dina's office in the diocese entered into a contract with a Catholic organization to help facilitate a particular conference. Dina and her diocesan team discerned that it would be best if the speakers at the conference represented the diversity of ethnicities that make up the Diocese of Baton Rouge. When she and her team presented this desire to the Catholic organization they were working with, they were informed that they might not be able to provide speakers of color. Upon doing research, Dina discovered the names of numerous speakers of color and presented them to the organization that was planning the conference. She made it clear that if the speakers did not represent Baton Rouge's diverse population, then the diocese would be unable to continue collaborating with their organization. In the end, the conference team was able to get the first choice that Dina and her team had requested. This one-day conference ended up being a huge success and bore much supernatural fruit within the Diocese of Baton Rouge.

When organizing conferences, retreats, and workshops, we can make sure that the content is relatable to all participants even if we cannot schedule speakers from diverse backgrounds. For example, as we share the gospel, we can relate certain aspects of our stories back to the lives of the saints from all over the world. If our message is about sexual abuse, we can share the story of St. Josephine Bakhita, who was an African slave. If our witness is about the "father wound," we can incorporate the story of St. Martin de Porres into our testimony. If we are addressing overcoming habitual sins and addictions, we can present the life of Chinese martyr St. Mark Ji Tianxiang. If we are offering a workshop on celibacy, we can share the witness of joyful celibates, such as the first Native American saint, Kateri Tekakwitha.

In addition to sharing the lives of the saints, it is important to know the people in our audience and what they are experiencing in their daily lives. Even if you do not feel equipped to speak on issues that disproportionately affect minorities (e.g., educational opportunities, unjust prison sentences, etc.), we can still offer petitions related to these issues during the intercessory prayers at Mass during these events.

Perspective Matters

Finally, when it comes to the educational materials we use to form our adults or youth in our communities, we can bring much more richness and inspiration to our students if we offer resources from a diverse group of Catholic authors, theologians, saints, and mystics. Dr. Drew Hart, a Black Protestant theologian, describes an interaction he had with a fellow Protestant pastor that sheds light on the neglect Christians suffer when formation materials are limited to resources with only one cultural perspective. The truth is the same in every culture, but it is not limited to one culture's way of expressing it.

One afternoon, Dr. Hart was invited by a white suburban pastor to meet for a beverage and dialogue with each other across the racial divide. They shared stories with each other about their church experience, seminary formation, and personal journeys with Christ.

At some point in the conversation, the suburban pastor grabbed a foam cup containing sweet tea and put it on the table between them. He said, "Drew … this cup has writing on my side of the cup and a logo on yours … I can't see what is on your side of the cup. Likewise, you can't see what is on my side of the cup. Because I can't see what is on your side of the cup, I need you to share with me your perspective so I can see things from your standpoint. Likewise, you need me to share my point of view so that you can understand the world from my vantage point."[77]

Dr. Hart expressed his gratitude to him for his well-intentioned gesture but explained that, unlike him, he actually did know a lot about what was on the other side of the cup. He said,

> I have learned history written from a white perspective. I have read white literature and poetry. I have learned about white musicians and artists. I have had mostly white teachers and professors through every stage of my educational process. I have read lots of white authors and have heard white intellectuals give lectures on a variety of topics. I have been inundated by white-dominated

and controlled television and media. I have lived
in a mostly white suburban community, and I have
lived on a predominantly white Christian campus.
The truth of the matter is that I wouldn't have been
on track to do a PhD without becoming intimately
familiar with the various ways that white people
think. My so-called success means that I have had to
know what it takes to meet white standards, whether
they are formal or informal.[78]

He continued to share with the suburban pastor that, unlike
him, he could probably go through his whole life without
needing to know Black literature, Black intellectual thought,
Black wisdom, Black art, or Black history, and he would not
be penalized for it.

As we seek to know each person as a member of the body of
Christ, we must always remember that individual people are
unique, made in God's image. Dr. Hart's words should not be
taken to mean that curricula can substitute for intentional
relationships. Knowing about European culture can never
substitute for getting to know the thoughts and desires of
each person we encounter within that culture, and knowing
about diverse cultures can never substitute for spending
time forming intentional relationships and actively listening
to each person within the African American community or
another diverse community.

To Dr. Hart's point, however, it would be a huge gift if our
Catholic schools, religious education programs, and adult
formation groups learned history, read literature, studied
theology, and prayed with insights from Americans of African
descent, Asian descent, and South American descent, as well
as the works written by those of European descent. It would
give all Catholics a richer understanding of the universality of
our Faith—and go far in healing the wound of racial division
in our Church and nation.

All of these efforts must have the ultimate goal of inspiring people to a deeper relationship with Jesus. To be intentional about inviting people from all races and ethnicities to join us in the presence of Jesus Christ in the Blessed Sacrament, let us make sure that the environment we are inviting them to enter is a bridge rather than a barrier.

CHAPTER 8

Accompanying the Body of Christ

There is a traditional Tanzanian parable about the dangerous outcomes that can arise when good people with good intentions do not listen to the people they are trying to help. This parable describes two groups of animals faced with surviving the dangerous floods of an excessively rainy season.

To avoid drowning, some fled up to the hills, while the agile monkeys were able to climb high into the treetops. As they rested in the trees, one of the monkeys looked down into the waters and saw a number of fish. He turned to a fellow monkey and said, "Look down, my friend. Look at those poor creatures. They are going to drown. Do you see how they struggle in the water?" The monkey's companion agreed and diagnosed that the fish were probably late in escaping to the hills and were now suffering the consequences. He asked, "How can we help them?" They decided that the best course of action would be to get close to the waters and pull the fish out, one by one.

Even though the task was difficult, the monkeys were able to successfully take all of the fish out of the water. Initially, the fish seemed to resist but, once they were laid on the ground, they appeared to rest very peacefully. One of the monkeys said, "They were trying to escape from us because they did not understand our good intentions. But when they wake up, they will be grateful." The other monkey commented, "Had it not been for us, all of these fish would have drowned." After a while, the monkeys began to realize that the fish were not going to wake up from their sleep. They saw that the fish had died. Their intention to "help" the fish was good but misguided.

This parable reveals how tragic it can be when individuals and groups do not take the time to listen, believe, and get to know those they are attempting to help. Conversely, if we walk close to others—if we are "proximate" to them—we can better serve them. This was the model Jesus used. He was close to the people with whom he shared his message. He leaned into those he served. He listened well to all those with whom he came in contact. He "emptied" himself so that everyone could be invited into a relationship with him and become an intentional member of his mystical body, the Church.

I sincerely believe that if all Catholics approached everyone in their parish borders as members of the body of Christ— or as people whom God is calling into relationship with the Church—then we would want to get to know every person who we encounter in our walk toward eternity. This is what happened to the twentieth-century English author and mystic Caryll Houselander while traveling on a train one day.

Houselander recounts that, while sitting on a crowded train, she noticed all of the diverse riders who had been thrown together as they headed to work or home.

> Quite suddenly I saw with my mind, but as vividly
> as a wonderful picture, Christ in them all. But I saw
> more than that; not only was Christ in every one
> of them, living in them, dying in them, rejoicing in
> them, sorrowing in them—but because he was in
> them, and because they were here too, here in this
> underground train, not only the world as it was at
> that moment, not only in all the countries of the
> world, but all those people who had lived in the
> past, and all those yet to come. I came out into the
> street and walked for a long time in the crowds. It
> was the same here, on every side, in every passer-by,
> everywhere—Christ.[79]

In his letter to the Galatians, St. Paul writes that, in baptism, we are incorporated into the one body of Christ: "For as many of you as were baptized into Christ have put on Christ. There is neither Jew nor Greek, there is neither slave nor free, there is neither male nor female; for you are all one in Christ Jesus" (Galatians 3:27–28).

One important goal of discipleship is to see the world through the eyes of Jesus. When he looks at baptized members of his body, Jesus sees himself. In the Acts of the Apostles, St. Luke describes the persecution the early Church endured at the hands of Saul, including the stoning of the Church's first martyr, Stephen.

While on his way to Damascus to persecute the Christians there, St. Paul hears a voice from above. It is Jesus, who says to him, *"Saul, Saul, why do you persecute me?"* (Acts 9:4, emphasis added). Notice that Jesus does not ask, *"Saul, Saul, why do you persecute my disciples?"* or *"Saul, Saul, why do you persecute my Church?"* Rather, Jesus identifies himself with his followers and asks, *"Why do you persecute me?"*

Through baptism, we literally become members of the body of Christ, the Church. We become one with him. Regardless of our race or ethnicity, we enter into a relationship with Jesus and the Church, his body. When heaven sees us, they see Jesus' body.

"Who Are You?"

A number of years ago, I went on an eight-day silent retreat under the direction of a holy priest named Msgr. John Esseff. He had served as a confessor for St. Teresa of Calcutta, an exorcist for the Diocese of Scranton, and a spiritual directee of St. Pio of Pietrelcina (Padre Pio).

During our first meeting, he asked me, "Who are you?" Of course, I could have responded in a number of ways: I am a priest. I am a pastor. A son. A brother. A sinner. I am broken. I am blessed. At first, I was not sure what he was getting at. Each day of the retreat, though, he asked me the same question. Msgr. Esseff would look into my eyes and pierce my soul with this question: "Who are you?" So each day, I would spend several hours with Jesus in prayer, asking the Lord to reveal to me the core of my identity, saying aloud the words, "Jesus, who am I?"

In prayer, I was eventually drawn to a scene in the Gospel of Matthew when Jesus was baptized by John the Baptist in the Jordan River. As I prayed with this image of Jesus' baptism, I saw myself in his place. I then heard the Father proclaim his blessing over me, "This is my beloved Son, with whom I am well pleased" (Matthew 3:17). The Holy Spirit revealed to me that I am the Father's beloved son. When the Father sees me, he sees Jesus, in whom he delights. The Father delights in me?! Whoa!

At my next meeting with Msgr. Esseff, I joyfully told him, "I know who I am! I am the Father's beloved son! I am the body of Christ! The Father delights in me!" He looked at me with a huge smile on his face, rubbed his beard like a wise man, and said, "That's right. That's who you are. You are the body of Jesus Christ!"

Our Identity in Jesus

Even though my retreat experience with Msgr. Esseff was life-changing, at some point I forgot this truth about my identity. I forgot that I am a beloved son of the Father. Some Christian commentators call this "spiritual amnesia." To continually remind myself of who I am in the eyes of God, I pray these words daily: "God, help me to see myself the way you see me. God, help me to know myself the way you know me. God, help me to love myself the way you love me."

It is not enough, though, for me to just focus my attention on how God sees me. As a disciple of Jesus Christ, I must always ask the Lord to help me to see others through his eyes as well. So I also recite these words each day: "God, help me to see others the way you see them ... God, help me to know others the way you know them ... God, help me to love others the way you love them."

Everything in our lives will change when we begin to see ourselves and others the way that God sees us. If I truly see each person as known and loved by God—and as a necessary member of our community—then I will want to imitate God and get to know and love him or her.

St. Thomas Aquinas teaches that love is "to will the good of another" (see CCC 1766).[80] The ultimate good is a personal relationship with Jesus Christ and the eternal salvation he offers. Therefore, if I am going to accompany the people in the geographical boundaries of my parish in their relationship with Jesus and his Church, then I need to find out what barriers exist that keep us from abiding in this relationship together.

Walking with the Word

Bible studies are so important for our work of evangelization. When we closely and consciously walk with a variety of people—persons from different ethnicities—who live within the boundaries of our parish, we open ourselves up to communal transformation in Christ. The more we share what Jesus is doing in our heart, through Scripture, the more we begin to open up other aspects of our lives with those with whom we are journeying. Some sharing will be joyful, and some will be about our struggles.

After listening to the hurts our brothers and sisters in Christ have experienced, we are encouraged to join together in prayer—taking these petitions to Jesus. He will have the answers and healing that we all need. When we share everything with Jesus in prayer, we are actually imitating Jesus, who shared everything with his Father in prayer all throughout the Gospels.

I learned this practice as a seminarian. One of my spiritual directors, Msgr. William Fitzgerald, frequently reminded me to communicate with Jesus before I ministered to people. In his own life, he followed this principle by refusing to answer the phone the first time anyone called, allowing all calls to go straight to voicemail. When a caller received his voicemail, he or she would hear, "You have reached Msgr. Fitz! I want you to know that you are very important to me, and so is your reason for calling. But I want you to know, if you have not spent time talking to Jesus about whatever it is you want to talk with me about, it would be best for you to hang up the phone right now, pray, and then call me back after you have gone to Jesus first! God bless you, and I cannot wait to hear from you!"

One of the ways Msgr. Fitz taught me to pray was a method called **ARRR**, which is an acronym for **A**cknowledge, **R**elate,

Receive, and **R**espond.

When communicating with Jesus, you are invited to do the following:

1. **A**cknowledge your thoughts, feelings, and desires.

2. **R**elate your thoughts, feelings, and desires to our Lord.

3. **R**eceive from your Lord by spending time with him in the Sacred Scriptures.

4. **R**espond to his Word with a concrete action.

The Witness of Katharine Drexel

One of the great American saints who turned to God day and night in her ministry with Native Americans and African Americans was St. Katharine Drexel. Mother Drexel was born into a wealthy Catholic family in 1858. Her father's estate was worth an estimated $400 million in today's dollars. Katharine was raised by her parents to have a deep and abiding relationship with Jesus through prayer and service to the poor. These works, though, were initially done "at a distance."

As an adult, she was moved by a book she read, *A Century of Dishonor* by Helen Hunt Jackson, on how Black people and Native Americans had been cruelly treated in the United States. St. Katharine learned about how the American government had taken advantage of Native Americans and forced them to live in terrible conditions. After being enlightened by her studies, she spent time with Native Americans in their communities and experienced their plight firsthand.

Devoted to her spiritual life, she shared her concerns with Jesus in the Blessed Sacrament, and from her prayer, she was inspired to share her thoughts and desires with the pope.

Upon receiving an audience with Pope Leo XIII, Katharine told him what she had learned. She impressed upon the Holy Father the need for missionaries to serve Jesus in people of color and the Native peoples of America. Leo XIII responded to her request by telling Katharine that she had the necessary gifts to serve these groups. He said, "Why not, my child, you yourself become a missionary?"[81]

After this encounter with the Holy Father, Katharine went to the Lord in prayer and sensed a confirmation of this missionary calling. She would go on to found a religious order, the Sisters of the Blessed Sacrament. Under her leadership, this religious community flourished with vocations, and a great impact was made on the lives of Native and African Americans thanks to the work and prayer of these holy sisters.

Following St. Katharine's model, our outreach to the people who live in our community begins by getting to know them. Once we have come to know the people in our community, we are invited to discern what resources we have in our toolboxes that best match their needs. I propose we limit our discernment of services to three areas: supernatural charisms, natural talents, and unearned privileges.

SUPERNATURAL CHARISMS

Supernatural charisms are "particular gifts that the Holy Spirit distributes 'as he wishes'" (1 Corinthians 12:11).[82] These charisms are referred to throughout the writings of the New Testament, the early Church Fathers, and the saints. St. Paul discusses some of these charisms in his first letter to the Corinthians:

> Now there are varieties of gifts, but the same Spirit;
> and there are varieties of service, but the same
> Lord; and there are varieties of working, but it is
> the same God who inspires them all in every one. To
> each is given the manifestation of the Spirit for the

> common good. To one is given through the Spirit the
> utterance of wisdom, and to another the utterance of
> knowledge according to the same Spirit, to another
> faith by the same Spirit, to another gifts of healing
> by the one Spirit, to another the working of miracles,
> to another prophecy, to another the ability to
> distinguish between spirits, to another various kinds
> of tongues, to another the interpretation of tongues.
> All these are inspired by one and the same Spirit,
> who apportions to each one individually as he wills.
> (1 Corinthians 12:4-11)

In his *Summa Theologica*, St. Thomas Aquinas elaborates on the writings of St. Paul concerning charisms. He explains that the charisms are bestowed on people so that they can cooperate in the justification of others.[83] In basic terms, charisms are gifts of the Holy Spirit given to us at baptism to be shared for the good of others.

One can discern a charism based on three criteria:

1. The charism is always used for the sake of others.

2. The charism bears supernatural fruit in the lives of others.

3. The charism is consistent over a long period of time.[84]

One of St. Katharine Drexel's supernatural charisms was intercessory prayer. This charism "empowers the sustained, intense prayer of a Christian for others as the means by which God's love and deliverance reaches those in need."[85] Catholics and other Christians who have this charism tend to receive miraculous responses from God to their prayers.

Upon founding the Sisters of the Blessed Sacrament, St. Katharine Drexel presented her sisters with a rule of life that instructed them to work for social justice for Native and African Americans and to pray before the Blessed Sacrament to sustain their works of evangelization, charity, and justice.

St. Katharine spent two hours every day on her knees in Adoration before Jesus in the Blessed Sacrament, praying that the efforts of her sisters would bear fruit.[86] This fruit would be seen many times, including one instance during a serious conflict with the Ku Klux Klan.

In Beaumont, Texas, as in other areas of the South, the KKK was openly persecuting African Americans. Upset with the work of St. Katharine and her sisters, the KKK posted a sign outside a Beaumont Catholic church that read, "We want an end of services here. We will not stand by while white priests consort nigger wenches in the faces of our families. Suppress it in one week, or flogging and tar and feathers will follow ... If people continue to come to this church, we will dynamite it."[87]

Many were terrified because the KKK had already tarred and feathered a Black parishioner. While the African American Catholics loved the parish and wanted their children to attend the parish school, the threats scared some away from attending Mass and receiving the sacraments. Instead of engaging these domestic terrorists, St. Katharine invited her sisters to prayer before the Blessed Sacrament. She believed the Lord would fight for any oppressed people since he proclaimed so throughout the Scriptures.

Shortly after St. Katharine and her sisters prayed on behalf of the persecuted African Americans in the parish, a tornado came and wiped out the local KKK headquarters. As a result, the KKK in Beaumont ceased its harassment, and the Black people of the parish returned to worship and continued to grow in their relationship with Jesus in the sacramental life of the Church.

NATURAL TALENTS

Natural talents are gifts that one can develop over the course of his or her life. One can be born with a natural athletic ability, but this gift needs to be developed over time through disciplined practice and workouts. In St. Katharine's case, she had a natural talent with numbers and financial matters, which she honed with the help of her uncle, Anthony Drexel. This would later help her make wise investments to acquire property to use in her order's mission to Native and African Americans.[88]

On one occasion, St. Katharine planned to purchase a large house in a segregated white neighborhood and convert it into a school for African American girls. Working with a lawyer, the property was bought for $25,000, and the deed was turned over to the Sisters of the Blessed Sacrament. When the white citizens of the neighborhood discovered who had bought the property—and what its intended use was—they sued the Blessed Sacrament sisters in an effort to stop the school from being established. Using her natural wits, St. Katharine was able to win the case and open her school for girls.[89] She would eventually found many more schools and universities, including Xavier University in New Orleans, the only historically Black Catholic university in the United States. Servant of God Sister Thea Bowman (1937–1990), an African American nun whose cause for canonization has been opened, served as a professor at Xavier University's Institute for Black Catholic Studies.

PRIVILEGE

In addition to her supernatural charism of intercessory prayer and her natural talents at finances, St. Katharine was also the recipient of an unearned handout called privilege. A privilege is an unearned benefit we receive from our family or society at large. In Katharine's case, her privilege was inherited wealth. At the time of his death in 1885, her father had amassed a fortune of more than fifteen million dollars (which, adjusted for inflation, is equivalent to approximately

$430 million today). After $1.5 million was distributed to twenty-nine charities, the remainder of the estate was split among his three daughters, including Katharine.

As a religious sister, St. Katharine used her inherited wealth to assist other members of the body of Christ in their efforts to serve the needs of African and Native Americans. In 1934, she collaborated with the American Scottsboro Committee for the legal defense of nine Black teenagers who had been accused of kidnapping two white women. Eight of these nine Black defendants were condemned to death, even though one of the alleged victims had repudiated her testimony.[90]

St. Katharine was also a major supporter of the National Association for the Advancement of Colored People (NAACP). The mission of the NAACP in the early 1900s was to work for equality of rights before the law, get rid of racial prejudice among citizens in the United States of America, and promote justice in the court system, adequate education for Black children, and employment opportunities for people of color.[91] She supported this civil rights organization financially and assisted with its anti-lynching campaign. In addition to the NAACP, St. Katharine was a generous benefactor to other Catholic religious communities who served African Americans, including the Josephite priests and brothers and Venerable Henriette Delille's religious order of consecrated women, the Sisters of the Holy Family.

Clearly, St. Katharine lived out Jesus' words to the rich young man: "If you would be perfect, go, sell what you possess and give to the poor, and you will have treasure in heaven; and come, follow me" (Matthew 19:21). She gave all she had— financially, physically, and spiritually—so that all members of the body of Christ could fulfill their mission in the Church and the world. St. Katharine and her sisters worked tirelessly to make sure that all people could have an opportunity to receive a quality education and mature in their relationship with Jesus.

Discerning Our Charisms, Natural Talents, and Privileges

The Bible and Catholic theologians throughout history have spoken of charisms God bestows on particular members of the Church. The Catherine of Sienna Institute in Colorado Springs, an organization dedicated to helping people discern their specific charism(s), has identified charisms, including encouragement, hospitality, mercy, evangelism, prophecy, teaching, healing, leadership, wisdom, and knowledge, among others.[92] (See the appendix for the full list.)

As disciples of Jesus, we can discern our particular charism with the assistance of the Siena Institute's "Called and Gifted" program. When we begin to discover our charisms, we can begin to practice these supernatural gifts in collaboration with other members of the body of Christ who have charisms that complement our own.

In addition to our charisms being used in collaboration with—and for—others, we are called to use our natural talents to build up the kingdom of God. As we have seen, these gifts are particular aptitudes or abilities with which we have been born that we develop through practice. In the Catholic Church in America, some of our leaders in past centuries have used their gifts in powerful ways to help people of color.

Courageous Witness from an Archbishop and the Sisters of St. Joseph

Archbishop Joseph Rummel (1876–1964) was ordained a priest of the Archdiocese of New York in 1902. He served as a pastor in New York for more than twenty-five years. In

1935, he became the Archbishop of New Orleans, where he served the faithful for nearly thirty years. In the 1940s, two decades before the passage of the Civil Rights Act of 1964, he began desegregating churches, schools, and institutions in the Archdiocese of New Orleans. He writes,

> Ever mindful therefore, of the basic truth that our Colored Catholic brethren share with us the same spiritual life and destiny, the same membership in the Mystical Body of Christ, the same dependence upon the Word of God, the participation in the Sacraments, especially in the Most Holy Eucharist, the same need of moral and social encouragement, let there be no further discrimination or segregation in the pews, at the Communion rail, at the confessional and in parish meetings, just as there will be no segregation in the kingdom of heaven.[93]

Though his mission was just, Archbishop Rummel met substantial opposition from many Catholics of the archdiocese. Civic leaders, teachers, families, religious sisters and brothers, and even his own priests fought against his efforts to end segregation in God's Church.

Why is it that some Catholic leaders do not speak up for—and do—what is right regarding the racial division in our churches and our nation? One reason is that they fear controversy and the loss of financial support for their projects and endeavors. Because of his systemic reforms on issues of race, Archbishop Rummel was threatened by powerful Catholic donors and political leaders in their resistance to integration. Many lay Catholics of the archdiocese wrote letters to the Vatican, demanding his removal. Some even picketed outside of his episcopal residence, burning a cross on his front lawn. Though he experienced hatred and persecution, Rummel persevered. He loved God and his law more than the approval of men. The actions of Archbishop Rummel are a powerful witness of authentic discipleship. Like the work of St. Katharine Drexel, they show how one can use his natural gifts of leadership to effect change.

Like the good archbishop, the Sisters of St. Joseph (SSJ) in Louisiana also stood on the right side of history. They worked to bring about much-needed educational opportunities for African American students in the Archdiocese of New Orleans. Using their natural gifts of teamwork and collaboration, they peacefully fought for the education of students of color despite strong pushback from affluent Catholics in the archdiocese. In her book *River of Fire*, Sister Helen Prejean details how her sisters stood up for justice during the racially tense times of the early 1960s.

In 1962, when Archbishop Rummel announced his decision to desegregate the Catholic schools of New Orleans, the Sisters of St. Joseph developed a plan to implement this change at St. Joseph's Academy, an all-girls private high school, which they had founded in 1858 and had historically admitted only white female students. The sisters decided to admit any young Black women who applied for the 1962–1963 school year. As an initial appeasement to the white parents who resisted integration, most of the other Catholic schools in the archdiocese limited admission to just a few Black students. The Sisters of St. Joseph, however, actively went into the Black community and intentionally welcomed students of color from the elementary and high schools in the area. A large number of African American girls enrolled at St. Joseph's Academy as a result.

Like Archbishop Rummel, however, the sisters began to receive negative pushback from the parents of the children attending their school. Parents began to pull their daughters out of the school because it had become, in their words, a "nigger" school. These parents then placed their daughters in Catholic schools that had remained nearly all white, with only a few "token" Black students.

The Sisters of St. Joseph encouraged the principals of the other schools in the archdiocese to follow their example by opening their doors wide to Black students. The principal of St. Joseph's Academy, Sister Alice Marie, said to the other principals, "Don't you see what is happening? By having only a token number of Black students, you're contributing to 'white flight.'" She pointed out that if every Catholic school in the archdiocese had the same open-door admissions policy to Black students, then parents would not have any option if they wanted their children to have a Catholic education. She asked, "Isn't [ending segregation] what the gospel calls us to do?"

Unfortunately, the other principals would not listen to Sister Alice Marie's wise counsel. They were afraid of the KKK and did not want to be labeled a "communist institution" by the racist Citizens Council of New Orleans. Most of all, they were afraid parents would pull their children out of their schools and send them to public schools. They were also concerned about the financial impact such an exodus would have on their institutions. Ultimately, these fears held sway over the clear mandate of the gospel of Jesus.

Each year, an increasing number of African American students enrolled at St. Joseph's Academy—and each year, more and more white students withdrew from the school. Eventually, due to an overall decline in total enrollment and a lack of funding, the school closed in 1979.[94] I cannot help but think how many people of color could have become priests, religious, or lay leaders in the Church if it was not for the poor choices the Catholic principals made to exclude them from their schools throughout the archdiocese.

What's New Is Old

Nearly sixty years following the passage of the Civil Rights Act of 1964, certain racist practices and attitudes continue to be perpetuated by practicing Catholics. Archbishop Alfred Hughes addressed racism during his tenure shepherding the Archdiocese of New Orleans from 2002 to 2009. Using his natural gift of listening, he heard the stories of Black people of the archdiocese who were being alienated and discriminated against due to their race.

During his listening sessions, he became aware that there were country clubs and institutions that still did not permit Black members. Even more alarming, he learned that some of those clubs and institutions were financially supported by Catholic parishes, schools, and organizations who had paid for gatherings, social events, and fundraisers at these locations. Think about how African American parishioners felt when their pastors and fellow parishioners would spend parish contributions to financially support organizations that did not allow Black people to be members.

In response to what he had heard, Archbishop Hughes issued a pastoral letter in 2006 on racial harmony, "Made in the Image and Likeness of God." He challenged Catholics in the archdiocese to acknowledge the hidden ways that racism continued to be practiced in our nation today and how we can work together to fight this evil. He advised Catholics to "refrain from membership in clubs or organizations which are not open to a racially or culturally diverse membership."[95]

His call to action was transformative on many levels. Some of the racial division that had been perpetuated by white-only country clubs and organizations was resolved by them opening the doors to Black members. Black people and other non-white Catholics finally felt like their voices were being heard. Some Catholics who were not aware of the racist practices of these clubs now no longer supported them. Because of an archbishop's openness to hearing the stories of all of his flock, where disunity once weakened the Church in New Orleans, unity had become a possibility.

The Power of Privilege

In addition to using our charisms and natural talents to build the kingdom of heaven on earth, we can also use our privileges to help others in our community. Most of us enjoy some kind of privilege that others do not. We should not feel guilty about our privilege. In many cases, we have not done anything personally to receive the privileges we possess. However, once we realize how our society accommodates us and alienates others, we have a responsibility to use our privilege for the good of others.

One might benefit from one or several societal privileges, including *racial privilege, environmental privilege, ethnic privilege, religious privilege*, and *socioeconomic privilege*. Depending on the situation, any person can benefit from a certain type of privilege. This applies to both Black and white people as well as women and men.

Here is an example from my own life. As a biracial priest, I can benefit from a kind of *ethnic privilege* in that I am often accepted by both Black and white people. I am able to hang out at predominately Black barbershops, which are historically safe places for people of color that are located in predominantly Black neighborhoods. I can fit in, without my motives being questioned.

I vividly remember being given a ride to get my haircut by one of my white seminary classmates. When we arrived at the barbershop, he said that he would wait in the car. What happened next brought laughter to every man in the barbershop. As I was getting my haircut, some of the men in the barbershop saw him and began to murmur about the "suspicious white man" in his car in the parking lot. (Apparently, they had recently been harassed by some white undercover police officers). When I realized that it was my friend they were worried about, I quickly explained the situation. They were relieved, and we all had a good laugh. It certainly was an eye-opening experience for me to recognize my ethnic privilege in that circumstance.

An *environmental privilege* that I and many other Americans benefit from is being able-bodied. Most things in our society cater to able-bodied people. For example, most door handles and elevator buttons are placed at a height that is difficult for disabled people to reach. Some older buildings (i.e., those that were built before the passage of the Americans with Disabilities Act of 1990) that are more than one-story high only have stairs, and so are inaccessible to wheelchair-bound individuals. In addition, some older churches do not have ramps, which makes it extremely difficult for many disabled parishioners to participate in worship as lectors and altar servers.

Because I have a sister who is paralyzed, one of the first things I look for when I am assigned to a parish are its accommodations for disabled citizens, especially ramps. It is important that all who are disabled feel welcome in the parish on equal terms with the able-bodied people in our community. Without such accommodations, many disabled persons would need to be carried into the church to participate in worship.

I enjoy certain privileges in life because I am an able-bodied Catholic priest, and I have certain cultural advantages that others do not because of my social standing. Yet there are many instances when I do not benefit, due to racial privilege. Said plainly, my skin color is occasionally an issue.

Becoming Aware of Racial Privilege

In America, those who have historically benefited most from racial privileges have been white people. The concept of being called "white" did not come into prominence until people of European descent in what would eventually become the United States wanted to make distinctions between persons who had rights and benefits under the law and those who did not. Proximity to the racial category of "white" became the determining factor. Rather than identifying with their particular ethnic group (for example, Irish or Italian), people of European descent began to see themselves as belonging to the white race.

Are there instances in our nation where white people do not benefit from racial privilege? Certainly. But the United States is a society with majority white leadership, and, generally speaking, people tend to feel more comfortable with people of their own race. If a white person has had a difficult life, with numerous personal setbacks and struggles, being white still offers them some advantages that a person of color may not currently enjoy. The general acceptance of white people—in most situations—is simply the norm in our society at present.

For example, if a Black person is walking or driving in a predominantly white neighborhood, there is a chance that he or she will be questioned by the residents or pulled over by the police. In fact, this happened to retired bishop Edward Braxton of Belleville, Illinois.

Bishop Braxton, one of the few African American bishops in the United States, experienced racial prejudice and discrimination both as a young priest and as a bishop. In his 2015 pastoral letter "The Racial Divide in the United States," he writes,

> I have had two personal experiences with law enforcement officers that made me very conscious of the fact that simply by being me, I could be the cause of suspicion and concern without doing anything wrong. The first experience was when I was a young priest. The second was when I was already a bishop. In both cases I was not in clerical attire. I was dressed informally.
>
> In the first experience, I was simply walking down a street in an apparently all-white neighborhood.

A police car drove up beside me and the officer asked, "What are you doing in this area? Do you live around here? Where is your car? You should not be wandering around neighborhoods where you do not live." I never told him I was a Catholic priest, but I wondered what it was I was doing to attract the attention of the officer? This was long before I heard the expression, "walking while black."

In the second experience, I was driving in my car in an apparently all-white neighborhood with two small chairs in the back seat and a table in the partially open trunk tied with a rope. A police car with flashing lights pulled me over. The officer asked, "Where are you going with that table and those chairs?" Before I could answer, he asked, "Where did you get them?" Then he said, "We had a call about a suspicious person driving through the area with possibly stolen furniture in his trunk." I wondered what I was doing to make someone suspicious. Many years would pass before I would hear the expression "racial profiling."[96]

Statistically, people of color are no more likely to break traffic laws than whites. However, they are much more likely to be stopped by police, and searched, ticketed, and even arrested.[97]

It is important for Catholic leaders to understand that racial privilege can be traced largely to generational racism—that is, the legacy of slavery, racial terrorism, and segregation under Jim Crow laws—and to current indirect racist institutional practices and policies. If it continues to go unchallenged, racial privilege will continue to perpetuate the racial divide both in our nation and even in our Church.

To be clear, possessing racial privilege does not mean that white people necessarily have easy lives, nor does it mean that people of color do not have privilege in many circumstances. Every human being has struggles and difficulties, simply by being born into a fallen world, and there are biases that take place with all races. In my experience, racial privilege does mean, though, that a white person does not suffer difficulties *because of his or her race* as does a person of color.

It is a privilege to be able to shop without being followed by security, drive without being pulled over by law enforcement for no reason, receive more job interviews because one's name does not "sound Black," get accepted into schools due to one's family lineage, or being discriminated against when trying to rent an apartment or buy a house despite having the appropriate financial situation and credit to do so.

If disciples of Christ recognize that they are benefiting from racial privileges while others are being placed at a disadvantage simply due to the color of their skin, then they are encouraged to suffer with those who are suffering. At a minimum, we are invited to take the sufferings of our brothers and sisters to God in prayer, as well as ask the Holy Spirit what action—big or small—we should take to stand in solidarity with those who face discrimination.

As daunting as this challenge may be, we can find strength in the knowledge that we "stand on the shoulders of giants"— on the work of those Christians throughout history who used their gifts, talents, and privileges to build up the kingdom of heaven on earth. Like them, if we really desire to follow Jesus faithfully, then we must pray for the grace to be courageous. We must follow the model of Christ and get close to the people of every race, nation, tribe, and tongue in our community. We are invited to listen to each other's stories, learn from one another, pray together, and work as a team of disciples so as to cultivate a civilization of love.

CHAPTER 9

At the Table with the Body of Christ

It has been said that God raises up specific saints throughout salvation history to combat specific evils. I have also been taught that, within the boundaries of every parish, there are members—and potential members—of the body of Christ who have the gifts that are needed to build up the kingdom of God.

In a conversation about how we could collaborate together better as a faith community to build a civilization of love, I learned about a parish experiencing supernatural fruit in their outreach. They did this because the members of their parish teams first discerned their individual charisms. They came to see and believe in the role each of them was called to play in the body of Christ.

Once each individual identified his or her particular charism, they began to pray as a group about how to apply these gifts to the specific needs in their community. They concluded that they were called to stand up against the evil being done by an abortion clinic located within the borders of the parish. It was the source of great wounding—to the mother, child, and others in the mother's life. The pastor and his team began to pray about the best way they could address this evil in their community.

After a period of prayer and discernment, they decided to gather as a pastoral team every Saturday and split up into groups based on their charisms. Those who had the charism of hospitality arrived early to set up the environment at the parish center. They made sure the center was warm and welcoming and had food for the other disciples. They enjoyed a time of fellowship and prayer before departing to their missions. Those with the charism of intercessory prayer went to the Adoration chapel and began to intercede for the conversion of hearts at the abortion clinic—the doctors, the clinic workers, and the women who were scheduled to receive abortions.

Others who also had the charism of intercessory prayer but who were more extroverted went to the clinic and prayed the Rosary. Still others had the gift of encouragement, and they would offer loving counsel to the women arriving at the clinic to have an abortion. If one of the women changed her mind about having an abortion, she was introduced to a team member who possessed the charism of mercy. This disciple would journey with the mother over the weeks and months ahead, offering her spiritual, emotional, and financial assistance. Back at the parish, the disciples who had the charism of prophecy spent their morning writing letters to state lawmakers in an attempt to have the abortion clinic shut down.

After a full morning's work at the clinic, the entire team gathered together again in the parish center for a meal and fellowship put together by the hospitality ministers. The pastor would then offer these faithful disciples a blessing before they went on their way.

Notice how this group of disciples operated. They first learned the needs in their community, and then they discerned their charisms. Aware of their limitations, they leaned on each other and collaborated as a team of disciples to address the evil of abortion. No one person tried to do everything. Everything was done as a collaborative effort, utilizing each person's particular charism.

This is the model St. Paul lays out for us in his first letter to the Church in Corinth:

> The body does not consist of one member but of many. If the foot should say, "Because I am not a hand, I do not belong to the body," that would not make it any less a part of the body. And if the ear should say, "Because I am not an eye, I do not belong to the body," that would not make it any less a part of the body. If the whole body were an eye, where would be the hearing? If the whole body were an ear, where would be the sense of smell? But as it is, God arranged the organs in the body, each one of them, as he chose. If all were a single organ, where would the body be? As it is, there are many parts, yet one body. (1 Corinthians 12:14–20)

As we have seen, sins of racism have divided the body of Christ throughout history and continue to cause division today. As disciples of Jesus, we are individually and collectively equipped with the charisms, natural talents, and resources needed to combat the evil of racism and bring about unity in the Church.

God created each of us for this time. We are the members of the body of Christ chosen now to combat this evil in our land. If each of us lives out our charism and shares our talents and resources for the good of our brothers and sisters, we can together heal hearts and reform minds. We can correct bad practices and prejudicial policies that perpetuate division in the Church and in our communities. We can be used by the Holy Spirit to console the heart of Jesus and foster unity among his disciples. In the presence of our Eucharistic Lord and Savior, we can all truly be one, imaging here on earth that diverse communion of saints in heaven!

Three Practical Ways to Engage

There are concrete, practical ways disciples of Jesus from different racial backgrounds can work together to heal the wounds of racism in our Church and nation. Some of these have already been discussed in this book. Here are some additional ideas.

I have divided these helpful suggestions into three categories: *Learn*, *Pray*, and *Act*.

LEARN

- **Visit "ground zero."** Reading about places and events is great, but nothing is as powerful as actually seeing them with your own eyes. I propose that you visit the Equal Justice Initiative's Legacy Museum, located on the site of a former warehouse in Montgomery, Alabama, where enslaved Black people were imprisoned. The museum offers its visitors an educational experience through the use of media, sculptures, videos, and exhibits that tell the story of the slave trade, racial terrorism, the Jim Crow South, and the world's largest prison system.

  Another powerful museum is the Whitney Plantation in Wallace, Louisiana. This museum is devoted to telling the true story of slavery in the southern United States. People today can be so dazzled by the physical beauty of a plantation that they forget what a plantation actually was—a slave labor camp, a place where African Americans were beaten, whipped, raped, tortured, lynched, and worked literally to death in many cases.

If one were to visit a Nazi concentration camp, such as Auschwitz in Poland, the preserved environment offers a space to mourn the atrocities that happened there to Jews, Catholics, and other minorities at the hands of their oppressors. Though most plantations disregard their history and downplay the evil that happened on their land, the Whitney Plantation tells the whole story and offers its visitors a sacred space to learn the untold stories of the people of color who endured unimaginable sufferings there and on similar plantations throughout the South.

- **Read about the Black Catholic experience.** If we are to seek to bridge the racial divide in our Church and country, we must know the stories of people of color. While nothing can take the place of building personal, intentional relationships with African Americans in our communities, these books give a much-needed perspective.

   ○ *The History of Black Catholics in the United States* by Fr. Cyprian Davis, OSB

   ○ *Desegregating the Altar: The Josephites and the Struggle for Black Priests, 1871–1960* by Stephen J. Ochs

   ○ *From Slave to Priest: A Biography of the Reverend Augustus Tolton (1854–1897): First Black American Priest of the United States* by Caroline Hemesath

   ○ *Black Catholics on the Road to Sainthood* by Michael Heinlein

- *The African American Catholic Youth Bible* by the National Black Catholic Congress

In addition to these books, the United States Conference of Catholic Bishops (USCCB) offers a number of resources at usccb.org/racism that address the sin of racism, including:

- "Open Wide Our Hearts: The Enduring Call to Love—A Pastoral Letter Against Racism," 2018
- "The Racial Divide in the United States," Bishop Edward K. Braxton, 2015
- "A Pastoral Letter on Racial Harmony," Archbishop Alfred C. Hughes, 2006
- "Love Thy Neighbor as Thyself, US Catholic Bishops Speak Against Racism," 2001
- "What We Have Seen and Heard: A Pastoral Letter on Evangelization," the Black Bishops of the United States, 1984
- "Brothers and Sisters to Us," US Catholic Bishops Pastoral Letter on Racism, 1979

- **Apply to Xavier University's Institute for Black Catholic Studies.** Xavier University was founded by St. Katharine Drexel. It is the only historically Black Catholic university in the United States, and it is where Servant of God Sister Thea Bowman served as a faculty member. Many Black and white leaders who serve in the African American community were formed in this institution.

PRAY

- **Worship at a predominantly African American Catholic church on a Sunday.** If you can regularly visit a predominantly Black parish for Sunday Mass and other formation events, do so. If not, then do so at least once. Why? The best way you can grow in a relationship with other brothers and sisters in the body of Christ is to worship alongside them. Your African American brothers and sisters have wisdom and insights that can help you as you work to build a civilization of love and form disciples of Jesus Christ within the boundaries of your parish.

- **Take Rosary walks.** In addition to worshipping God with people of different ethnicities, consider taking Rosary walks with diverse groups of disciples through different neighborhoods in your parish. The devil hates the Rosary! Imagine how many hearts can be changed through your prayers—and how you could inspire others in your area to console the heart of Jesus by praying together to heal racial division.

- **Create a personalized "Litany of Saints."** Litanies are powerful prayers that invoke the intercession of the holy men and women who stand before the face of God in heaven. What I am proposing here, though, is a twist on a traditional litany of saints—a prayer litany that features the names of any person you know.

Two possibilities are a "Litany of the Body of Christ" and a "Litany of the Image of God." These prayers will help remind you that every person is created in the image of God, and the body of Christ contains many baptized members who look different from us. If we see all of our neighbors as made in God's image, then the way we think about them, treat them, speak about them, and listen to them will be transformed—and we will walk alongside them as our brothers and sisters.

A Litany of the Body of Christ could include any person you know who is a baptized Christian. It could look like this:

- ○ *[Name] is the body of Christ.*

- ○ *[Name] is the body of Christ.*

- ○ *Etc.*

A Litany of the Image of God could include the names of anyone you know, whether they are a baptized Christian or not. It could look like this:

- ○ *[Name] is made in the image of God.*

- ○ *[Name] is made in the image of God.*

- ○ *Etc.*

- **Priests can offer a Mass of Reparation.** Throughout the history of the Church, Masses of Reparation have been offered for the sins committed by Catholic clergy, religious, and laity. One of these sins was the enslavement of an entire group based on their race. A day that is especially appropriate for Masses of Reparation is the nineteenth of June (or Juneteenth, as it is more commonly known), the day in 1865 when slaves in Texas learned of their emancipation from slavery. It would be a very powerful witness for the bishop of a diocese to celebrate this Mass annually in the cathedral church, with many of his priests concelebrating.

  At the end of a Mass of Reparation for the sins of slavery and racism, I propose that parishes recite the prayer to St. Michael the Archangel. Celebrating the Holy Sacrifice of the Mass is a powerful tool in combating the enemy, so we need the ongoing protection from St. Michael and the angels in the spiritual battle we are fighting.

- **Holy Hours of Reparation.** I invite priests to offer holy hours of reparation before the Blessed Sacrament.

During this period of Adoration, the priest or deacon can lead the congregation in praying the Rosary, or at least the Sorrowful Mysteries. You could adapt your Rosary to include prayers for racial reconciliation.

Here is an example of a Rosary with added prayers for racial reconciliation:

> Hail Mary, full of grace, the Lord is with thee. Blessed art thou among women, and blessed is the fruit of thy womb, Jesus ...

> *... whose sweat became like great drops of blood on the ground in the garden of Gethsemane because he knew that there would come a day when 10.7 million Black people would be kidnapped from West Africa and sold into slavery in North and South America. Lord God, I offer penance on behalf of the men and women who participated in the grave sin of human trafficking against the African men, women, and children who were created in your image.*

> Holy Mary, Mother of God, pray for us sinners, now and at the hour of our death. Amen.

- **Clergy, religious, and laity can offer their Liturgy of the Hours prayers.** I propose that those who pray the Divine Office offer up some of their daily Liturgy of the Hours for the African Americans who were terrorized with persecution, discrimination, and lynching following their emancipation from slavery.

ACT

From the Gospels, we know Jesus was devoted to contemplative prayer. He gave us an example of prayer when he spent forty days in the desert, when he went off to pray alone throughout his public ministry, and on the eve of his passion in the garden of Gethsemane, when he poured out his heart to his Father.

Together with this prayer, he took action. As his disciples, we are called to action as well.

Here are some hands-on ideas:

- **Reassess the policies of our Catholic schools.** If you are involved with Catholic education, then I would encourage you to collaborate with an ethnically diverse group of people and work together to review the written policies and practices of any school (or schools) under your purview. If you work with people from different racial backgrounds, then unintentional discriminatory practices may be brought to light that may otherwise go unnoticed.

- **Review school curricula.** In addition to reviewing policies that accommodate some and discriminate against others, I encourage you to review your school's religion curriculum, as well as that of your overall religious education program. Determine if it includes any content on the history of Black Catholics in the United States. If not, look into resources that are available and can be included in the curriculum in the future.

  One resource that is being used by a number of schools and religious education programs across the country is *Black Catholic History* by Kaye Crawford. The author is a graduate of Xavier University's Institute of Black Catholic Studies and was mentored by the late Fr. Cyprian Davis, the author of *History of Black Catholics*. This book provides young students of all races with tools that can help them begin to heal racial divisions.*

---

* Ascension, the publisher of this book, also has a number of faith formation series that feature a diverse group of evangelists and catechists, including Fr. Mike Schmitz, Paul J. Kim, Mari Pablo, Naomi Owens, Sister Miriam James, Dr. Ansel Augustine, Chika Anyanwu, and myself in its programs like *Chosen*, *Connected*, and *Venture*. In addition to these faith formation programs, Ascension Presents has

- **Go out and invite everyone in your parish to participate in your faith formation groups.** It is important to include diverse members of the body of Christ in your faith formation groups and studies. Everyone in your parish's boundaries needs to have the opportunity to grow in their relationship with Jesus and his Church. For example, look at your small group Bible study and ask, "Which groups of people are not represented here?" Go out of your comfort zone and reach out to them with an inviting spirit.

- **Purchase ethnically diverse images of the saints for your Catholic parishes and schools.** Incorporate diverse artwork, paintings, stained glass images, and statues of Jesus, Mary, Joseph, the angels, and the saints throughout your parish church and school campus. When you go out into your community and invite fallen-away Catholics and non-Catholics to spend time in your parish, make sure they feel welcome. Seeing holy images of saints from all races and ethnicities can go a long way toward this goal.*

---

free content on practical ways we can heal the racial divide through its YouTube channel and podcasts. This content includes my podcast *Ask Fr. Josh* and conversations I had with Jeff Cavins and Fr. Mike Schmitz, as well as with the Franciscan Friars of the Renewal.

*   Diverse images of holiness are available for purchase at the following websites: Portraits of Saints, National Black Catholic Congress, and Ascension Press.

- **Make sure people of color have a voice at the table.**
  It is important for people of color who are members of
  your parish community to have a voice at the leadership
  table. If your parish has a pastoral council, finance
  council, or missions and retreats team, be sure to invite
  people of color to be members. We cannot serve everyone
  in our parish borders if we are not intentionally listening
  to people from all the communities within it.

- **Lift up your voice.** If you feel called to a more prophetic
  role in the Church, then use your voice to denounce
  racism publicly whenever and wherever it raises its ugly
  head. If Catholics do not address the evils of racism
  that are still being manifested in our society through
  policies and practices, then those of us who are people
  of color will not feel safe in our local churches. Just as
  we publicly denounce the clergy sexual abuse scandal,
  we need to speak out against racism at our dinner
  table, in our neighborhoods, in our workplaces, in our
  social groups, or on our social media pages. Follow on
  social media Catholic people of color who are working
  for racial reconciliation and share their posts with the
  circles with which you have influence. As the Holocaust
  survivor Ellie Wiesel has famously said, "Neutrality helps
  the oppressor, never the victim. Silence encourages the
  tormentor, never the tormented."

- **Engage in peaceful protests.** In addition to using
  your voice, get plugged in with peaceful protests
  and marches against injustice. Planned Parenthood
  is the largest abortion provider in America, and its
  founder, Margaret Sanger, was a devout racist. In her
  lifetime, she advocated for the extermination of African
  Americans. Much like Black babies who are targeted
  in the womb, Black men and women have been the

targets of police brutality in the streets.* These acts of violence, both inside and outside of the womb, should rightfully inspire members of the body of Christ to protest and march against such grave injustices.

- **Financially support Black Catholic ministries and causes.** If you are financially able, I would invite you to donate money to predominantly Black Catholic parishes, schools, organizations, and the religious orders that serve them. Quite often, these communities are underfunded and lack much-needed resources. Making a sacrifice to financially assist the Sisters of the Holy Family, the Josephites, or the Oblate Sisters of Providence can help these devoted servants of Christ continue their mission to make disciples in predominantly Black and brown communities.

  You can also financially contribute to the cause of canonization for the six African American holy men and women who are on the path to sainthood. Your donations can help their causes move forward and spread their witness throughout the nation and the world, which could inspire a whole new generation of saints.

- **Join the Knights of Peter Claver and Ladies Auxiliary.** The Knights of Peter Claver, Inc., is a historically African American Catholic lay organization in the United States. The organization is named after St. Peter Claver, the missionary priest who ministered

---

* Here are just a few examples: In 1991, an infamous video shows Rodney King being beaten by a group of white police officers after a traffic stop; in 1999, after Mayor Rudy Guiliani promised to clean up the streets of New York, a young unarmed black man, Amadou Diallo, was shot forty-one times by four police officers while attempting merely to pull out his wallet; in 2010, Aiyana Stanley-Jones, a seven-year-old girl, was shot and killed by the police while sleeping in her bed after they entered her Detroit home during a drug raid; in 2020, George Floyd died at the hands of the Minneapolis police, as officer Derek Chauvin knelt on his neck for more than eight minutes as he was handcuffed. Sadly, the list could go on.

to the African slaves. This community has been forming disciples to serve the Church, assist the sick and disabled, and promote social and intellectual association of its members since 1909.

- **Attend the National Black Catholic Congress.** The NBCC is rooted in promoting the agenda for the evangelization of African Americans and improving the physical conditions for Black people in church and society. In the 1800s, Daniel A. Rudd, an African American Catholic, established the Colored Catholic Congress Movement. These congresses are critical for disciples of Jesus Christ who are seeking ongoing formation in the works of evangelization, catechesis, justice, and charity.

- **Avoid attending or financially supporting certain events.** Another prophetic action is to avoid participating in events and conferences that host speakers whose words do not welcome members of the Black community. Just as Archbishop Hughes influenced the country club to change its racist practice of not allowing Black members, Catholics have influence when it comes to which conferences we will attend and which events we will not.

All of these suggestions of how we can learn, pray, and act can be used by God to draw more people from every race and ethnicity to Jesus and the sacramental life of the Church. If we can abide together with our racially and ethnically diverse brothers and sisters—and with the unity found in the Eucharist, then we can remain in communion with Jesus. This will contribute to a peaceful, joyful, and spirit-filled sojourn here on earth, leading to the ultimate communion with each other in heaven.

CHAPTER 10

The Mission Continues for the Body of Christ

In the summer of 2010, I was able to spend some time alone with our Lord Jesus on an eight-day silent retreat in Omaha. It was an amazing experience to spend four intentional hours throughout the day—morning, afternoon, evening, and night— with the Sacred Scriptures and the Blessed Sacrament. From my youth, I have always enjoyed talking with people, but the joy I experienced in the silence of that retreat with the Lord totally rocked my world.

On the last day, I was in the chapel with my Bible, kneeling before the Eucharist. I remember praying, "God please, don't let the silence end. These past eight days have been too good. I don't want this intimacy with you to end."

I distinctly remember perceiving the presence of our Blessed Mother Mary. In the silence of my heart, I heard her say to me, "But, my son, with Jesus Christ, there is always so much more."

I was not sure if the voice I heard was really from that of the Blessed Virgin Mary or if it was simply my imagination.

Regardless, I did not have time to discern the voice's origin since the concluding Mass of the retreat was about to begin.

Msgr. Fitzgerald was the main celebrant that day for Mass. As you may recall, this is the priest who taught me to talk to Jesus before I talk to people. He was assigned to be my spiritual director for the remainder of the summer. He continued to serve as my spiritual director up until the day he passed away. He began Mass by saying, "I have been praying for all of you men during these past eight days. I can tell this retreat has been a gift for many of you. I want you to know that, as I prayed for you this morning, I perceived our Blessed Mother, the Virgin Mary, speak, and she told me to tell you, 'As good as this retreat has been, with Jesus Christ, there is always so much more.'"

So Much More

My purpose and hope with this book has been to point out a few things some may not have considered and to more intentionally engage these conversations within our Church. If we truly want to help fulfill the command of Jesus to "make disciples of all nations," we must not be blind to the sufferings of the Black community.

The words Msgr. Fitzgerald and I both perceived in prayer are important to keep in mind as we continue our walk with Jesus Christ. I believe we become settled in our spiritual life because we think our current situation will never improve. The same attitude can apply to our relationships with people. We settle for mediocrity or the status quo because we consider our possibilities limited or see our efforts showing little progress. Nowhere is this more evident than in our attempt to heal hearts and transform systems of racial injustice that create division in the body of Christ. However, as our Lady said, "With Jesus Christ, there is so much more."

We have certainly come a long way in healing the racial wounds and transforming the racially unjust systems that have divided our Church and country for so long. Yes, slavery and legalized segregation are a thing of the past. Some people of color are visible in positions of leadership in the Church, in society, and in government. These are certainly great strides. Even still, these advances should not cause us to settle for the status quo. We should fight the temptation to say how "good" things are today. There is more work to be done.

During slavery, I am sure there were many people, both in the North and the South, who thought this evil practice would never end. So they began to justify slavery with the myth of the "gentle" slave owner. This broken thinking allowed people to justify its continued existence and cease doing the hard work needed to eradicate it. Of course, a "gentle" slave owner is a contradiction in terms, as ownership of another human being is contrary to the dignity of each person and the teachings of Christ.

During the civil rights movement in the United States, there were groups of people, both white and Black, who had come to terms with the Jim Crow era and the reality of segregation, despite all threats, trauma, and tragedy. But Dr. King and many others were unwilling to settle for the existence of unjust laws; they refused to let go of their vision of what was essential to the survival of America—racial justice. Their moral compasses directed them to a higher personal morality.

Today, in a society historically many decades removed from the Jim Crow era, racism is publicly condemned, yet we continue to witness much evidence of ongoing racial division in America. This division can even be found in the Church, as members of the Black community are absent from our churches, and many Catholic leaders do not seem to see that they are missing.

We are called to see each person, of every race, as a member of the body of Christ or a potential member of the body of Christ. We are called by Jesus himself to go out to preach the good news of salvation to "every nation" so that each person may receive the great gifts God offers in his Word and sacraments. We are called to know Jesus and to be filled with the fire of his love so that we may follow the model he gave us and form intentional relationships with our brothers and sisters, inviting them to the greatest relationship—the relationship with Jesus in the Blessed Sacrament.

Who will step up to answer this call? The answer for a disciple of Jesus needs to be an unequivocal "I will!" But we cannot do these mighty and necessary works of justice unless we *lean in* to Jesus. He is the bestower of the gifts we need to accomplish his will to end the scourge of racism and evangelize all peoples.

Transformation

Imagine if every person spent intentional time with Jesus in the Blessed Sacrament. So many diverse saints in the two-thousand-year history of the Church were formed by God as they were on their knees before the Eucharist. St. Teresa of Calcutta speaks of this transformation when, in 1973, she and her Missionaries of Charity sisters began their daily holy hours and saw their community grow and flourish. She writes,

> In our congregation we would have adoration once a week for one hour. Later in 1973 we decided to have a daily hour of adoration. The work which we have to do is enormous. The homes that we have for the sick and dying destitute are completely full everywhere. But from the moment in which we began to have an hour of adoration each day, the love of Jesus became more intimate in our hearts, our charity among us was more understanding, and the love of the poor

> was full of compassion, and in this manner, our
> vocations doubled. The hour that we dedicate to
> Jesus in the Eucharist is the greatest moment of the
> day, it is what changes our hearts.[98]

All of us have the potential to be formed by Jesus in the Eucharist and used by him to heal hearts and transform lives, but only if we address the hidden barriers that keep so many people of different races from encountering our Eucharistic Jesus in this very powerful way. As St. John Paul II said, "The entire Church is in need of the transforming and sanctifying power of the Eucharist."

In the Gospel of Luke, we read about Jesus' journey toward Jerusalem. Traveling through Samaria and Galilee, he entered a village and met ten lepers. Their response is inspiring, and Jesus' response gives us hope.

> He was met by ten lepers, who stood at a distance
> and lifted up their voices and said, "Jesus, Master,
> have mercy on us." When he saw them he said to
> them, "Go and show yourselves to the priests."
> And as they went they were cleansed. Then one of
> them, when he saw that he was healed, turned back,
> praising God with a loud voice; and he fell on his
> face at Jesus' feet, giving him thanks. Now he was a
> Samaritan. Then said Jesus, "Were not ten cleansed?
> Where are the nine? Was no one found to return and
> give praise to God except this foreigner?" And he
> said to him, "Rise and go your way; your faith has
> made you well." (Luke 17:12–19)

Jesus always has more to give to us in our walk with him. Nine of the lepers received only a physical healing. The one who came back to spend time with Jesus, however, was able to receive more—a healing of his soul. This side of heaven, every one of us is in need of more healing and transformation. We receive healing and transformation through intentional time spent with the Lord. Once empowered, we can fruitfully share this healing with others.

The meditation "Prophets of a Future Not Our Own" offers us some hopeful words:

> It helps, now and then, to step back and take a long view. The Kingdom is not only beyond our efforts, it is even beyond our vision. We accomplish in our lifetime only a tiny fraction of the magnificent enterprise that is God's work. Nothing we do is complete, which is a way of saying that the Kingdom always lies beyond us. No statement says all that could be said. No prayer fully expresses our faith. No confession brings perfection. No pastoral visit brings wholeness. No program accomplishes the Church's mission. No set of goals and objectives includes everything. This is what we are about.
>
> We plant the seeds that one day will grow. We water seeds already planted, knowing that they hold future promise. We lay foundations that will need further development. We provide yeast that produces far beyond our capabilities. We cannot do everything, and there is a sense of liberation in realizing that. This enables us to do something, and to do it very well. It may be incomplete, but it is a beginning, a step along the way, an opportunity for the Lord's grace to enter and do the rest.
>
> We may never see the end results, but that is the difference between the master builder and the worker. We are workers, not master builders; ministers, not messiahs. We are prophets of a future not our own.[99]

As St. Paul reminds us, we do not need to do all of this work for God's kingdom on our own. Nor do we need to see all of our evangelization efforts through to the end. In his letter to the Church in Corinth, Paul teaches us that one member of the body of Christ plants the seeds, and another waters it—and God makes it grow in his way and time (see 1 Corinthians 3:7–9).

As we plant some seeds and water others, I encourage those of you who are white Catholics not to lose heart when you see fellow members of the body of Christ—even family and close friends—struggling with or rejecting the call to accompany people of color in discipleship. Consider the pain Jesus experienced in his agony in the garden of Gethsemane, as his apostles were seemingly clueless to the pain he was experiencing (see Matthew 26:36-46). Note that Jesus did not reject or abandon them simply because they were oblivious to his pained heart. As disciples of Christ, we need to pray for the grace to imitate him and not give up on our brothers and sisters when they do not support or even oppose the work we are doing for the kingdom of God.

For those of you who are Black Catholics, I invite you to look for ways to enter relationships with those who are seeking to heal racial division, and to continue to *lean in* to relationships with the six African Americans on the road to sainthood:

- Venerable Pierre Toussaint (1776-1853)

- Venerable Henriette Delille (1812-1862)

- Venerable Augustus Tolton (1854-1897)

- Servant of God Mary Lange (c. 1784-1882)

- Servant of God Julia Greely (c. 1833-1918)

- Servant of God Thea Bowman (1937-1990)

Their friendship with us can help us to remain in the sacramental life of the Catholic Church and bear supernatural fruits in our efforts to become saints and form saints in the geographical boundaries of our communities.

Finally, we should all pray for the grace to persevere as we labor here on earth in our walk toward eternity. Think of the glory we will experience when, at the end of our lives, we can say and pray the words, "Jesus, instead of choosing to do nothing, I chose to do something. I could not do everything. But Jesus, with your grace, I chose to do something so that our Father's will could be done on earth as it is in heaven."

Notes

1   *Catechism of the Catholic Church* (CCC) 107; *Dei Verbum* 11.

2   Martin Luther King Jr., interview on *Meet the Press*, NBC, April 17, 1960. A transcript of this interview is available at kinginstitute.stanford.edu/. The audio and video of this interview can also be found online.

3   Jeff and Emily Cavins, *Walking Toward Eternity: Engaging the Struggles of Your Heart* (West Chester, PA: Ascension, 2012), 88.

4   "St. Damien of Molokai," ewtn.com/.

5   Merridith Frediani, "Adoring the Eucharist Is About Relationship with God," Ascension Presents article, November 9, 2018, ascensionpress.com/.

6   St. Peter Julian Eymard, *La Presence re'elle (The Real Presence)*, vol. 1 (Paris: 1950), 270–271, 307–308.

7   Cyprian Davis, *The History of Black Catholics in the United States* (New York: Crossroad, 1995), 9–10.

8   St. John Chrysostom, "Homily III," in *Nicene and Post-Nicene Fathers, First Series*, vol. 9, ed. Philip Schaff (Buffalo, NY: Christian Literature Publishing Co., 1889), 359.

9   Quoted here is the meditation "Fall in Love." Though often
    attributed to Fr. Pedro Arrupe, Fr. Joseph Whelan has also
    been named as the writer of this meditation. The author of
    this book is citing its attribution to Fr. Arrupe in Paul Hoesing,
    Have I Been With You? Personal Prayer for Young Disciples
    (Huntington, NY: National Conference of Diocesan Vocation
    Directors, 2014), 13.

10 See Marie Justine Fritz, "Federal Housing Administration
    (FHA)," *Encyclopedia Britannica*, August 9, 2019,
    britannica.com/.

11 See Christine Tamir, "The Growing Diversity of Black America,"
    Pew Research Center (website), March 25, 2021,
    pewresearch.org/.

12 From Mother Teresa's "Varanasi Letter" (March 25, 1993),
    quoted in Joseph Langford, *Mother Teresa's Secret Fire*
    (Huntington, IN: Our Sunday Visitor, 2008), 54–55.

13 Fr. Tom Hopko, quoted in Thomas J. Neal, "Hopko-isms, Part 1,"
    Neal Obstat Theological Opining (blog), July 23, 2015,
    nealobstat.wordpress.com/.

14 Francis, *Evangelii Gaudium* (November 24, 2013), 24.

15 Craig S. Keener, *The Gospel of John: A Commentary*, vol. 1
    (Grand Rapids, MI: Baker Academic, 2003), 589–590.

16 Toni Morrison, interview by Stephen Colbert, *The Colbert
    Report*, November 19, 2014, cc.com/.

17 See Bryan Massingale, *Racial Justice and the Catholic Church*
    (Maryknoll, NY: Orbis, 2010), 46.

18 Quoted in Tom Neal, "'Listen Carefully ... and Incline the Ear
    of your Heart'—Rule of St. Benedict," *Word on Fire* (blog),
    July 11, 2017, wordonfire.org/.

19 Jason Evert, *Saint John Paul the Great: His Five Loves*
    (Lakewood, CO: Totus Tuus Press, 2014), 83.

20 James M. Washington, ed., *A Testament of Hope: The Essential
    Writings and Speeches of Martin Luther King Jr.* (New York:
    Harper One, 1986), 345–346.

21 M. Shawn Copeland, ed., *Uncommon Faithfulness: The Black Catholic Experience* (Maryknoll, NY: Orbis, 2009), 80.

22 John Paul II, Address to the Black Catholic Community of New Orleans (September 12, 1987), 5, original emphasis.

23 "What We Have Seen and Heard: A Pastoral Letter on Evangelization from the Black Bishops of the United States" (Cincinnati, OH: St. Anthony Messenger Press, 1984), 20, emphasis added.

24 Martin Luther King Jr., "At 11 a.m. Sunday morning," as cited in Deborah L. Hall, David C. Matz, and Wendy Wood, "Why Don't We Practice What We Preach? A Meta-Analytic Review of Religious Racism," *Personality and Social Psychology Review* 14, no. 1 (February 2010): 126–139.

25 Latasha Morrison, *Be the Bridge: Pursuing God's Heart for Racial Reconciliation* (Colorado Springs, CO: WaterBrook, 2019), 108–109.

26 Morrison, *Be the Bridge*, 111.

27 David Eltis and Paul F. Lachance, Estimates of the Size and Direction of Transatlantic Slave Trade (2010), at slavevoyages.org/.

28 John W. Blassingame, *The Slave Community: Plantation Life in the Antebellum South* (New York: Oxford University Press, 1979), 7.

29 Blassingame, *The Slave Community*, 249–283.

30 Wilma A. Dunaway, *The African-American Family in Slavery and Emancipation* (Cambridge: Cambridge University Press, 2003), 67–68.

31 Thomas A. Foster, "The Sexual Abuse of Black Men Under American Slavery," *Journal of the History of Sexuality* 20, no. 3 (September 2011): 447.

32 Jamie T. Phelps, ed., *Black and Catholic: The Challenge and Gift of Black Folk—Contributions of African American Experience and Thought to Catholic Theology* (Milwaukee, WI: Marquette University, 2002), 46.

33 Davis, *The History of Black Catholics in the United States*, 39.

34 Davis, 38–39.

35 Encyclopedia.com, s.v. "Delille, Henriette 1813–1862."

36 Virginia Meacham Gould, *Henriette Delille* (Strasbourg: Editions du Signe, 2012), 37–40.

37 Gould, *Henriette Delille*, 9.

38 Gould.

39 Gould, 10.

40 Gould, 56.

41 Phelps, *Black and Catholic*, 49.

42 Phelps.

43 Phelps, 48.

44 William Warren Rogers et al., *Alabama: The History of a Deep South State* (Tuscaloosa, AL: University of Alabama Press, 1994), 234.

45 Glen Feldman, *The Irony of the Solid South: Democrats, Republicans, and Race, 1865–1944* (Tuscaloosa, AL: University of Alabama Press, 2013), 5. See also Carl Schurz, Report on the Condition of the South by 1865, 39th Cong., 1st Sess. No. 2 (1865), 18.

46 Feldman.

47 "Factbox: Black US Senators and Governors," *Reuters* (June 29, 2008), reuters.com/.

48 Leon F. Litwack, *Been in the Storm So Long: The Aftermath of Slavery* (New York: Vintage Books, 1980), 267–277.

49 Allen W. Trelease, *White Terror: The Ku Klux Klan Conspiracy and Southern Reconstruction* (New York: Harper & Row, 1971), 3, 5.

50 Trelease, 95, 117, 120–122.

51 Richard Maxwell Brown, *Strain of Violence: Historical Studies of American Violence and Vigilantism* (New York: Oxford University Press, 1975), 214, 323.

52   Staff of the Equal Justice Initiative, *Lynching in America: Confronting the Legacy of Racial Terror*, 3rd ed. (Montgomery, AL: Equal Justice Initiative, 2017), 39–40.

53   Harold Burke-Sivers, *Father Augustus Tolton: The Slave Who Became the First African-American Priest* (Irondale, AL: EWTN, 2018), 9.

54   Burke-Sivers, 10.

55   Burke-Sivers.

56   Burke-Sivers, 11.

57   Burke-Sivers.

58   Burke-Sivers, 14.

59   Burke-Sivers, 16.

60   Burke-Sivers,18.

61   Stephen J. Ochs, *Desegregating the Altar: The Josephites and the Struggle for Black Priests, 1871–1960* (Baton Rouge, LA: Louisiana State University Press, 1990), 340–341.

62   Larry Peterson, "Despite Protests at His Ordination, He Was America's First Black Bishop of the 20th Century," *Atleteia*, February 26, 2019, aleteia.org/.

63   Francis, *Fratelli tutti* (October 3, 2020), 97, vatican.va/.

64   US Department of Health and Human Services, National Institute on Drug Abuse, NIH pub. No. 07-6205 (Bethesda, MD: 2007), 32, referenced in Michelle Alexander, *The New Jim Crow: Mass Incarceration in the Age of Colorblindness* (New York: The New Press, 2012), 7.

65   Alexander, *The New Jim Crow*, 1–2.

66   Alexander, 53.

67   Alexander, 53–54.

68   Meagan Flynn, "A 'Saggy Pants' Violation Led to a Fatal Police Chase," *Washington Post*, May 30, 2019, washingtonpost.com/.

69 Marianne Bertrand and Sendhil Mullainathan, "Are Emily and Greg More Employable than Lakisha and Jamal? A Field Experiment on Labor Market Discrimination" (working paper no. 9873, National Bureau of Economic Research, Cambridge, MA, 2003).

70 Ramos v. Louisiana, 580 U.S. (2020), https://www.supremecourt.gov/opinions/19pdf/18-5924_n6io.pdf.

71 Maura Hohman, "America's 1st Black Cardinal, Wilton Gregory, Opens Up About Experiences with Racism," *Today*, February 15, 2021, today.com/.

72 Thomas J. Neal, "No Humility No Holiness," *Neal Obstat Theological Opining* (blog), October 20, 2018, nealobstat.wordpress.com/.

73 Dennis Hamm, *Catholic Commentary on Sacred Scripture: Philippians, Colossians, Philemon* (Grand Rapids, MI: Baker Academic, 2013), 185.

74 Edward K. Braxton, "The Racial Divide in the United States: A Reflection for the World Day of Peace 2015" (January 1, 2015), 5.

75 Thomas Aquinas, *Summa Theologica* III.54.2

76 Celestine Cepress, ed., *Sister Thea Bowman, Shooting Star: Select Writings and Speeches* (Winona, MN: Saint Mary's Press, 1993), 34.

77 Drew G. I. Hart, *Trouble I've Seen: Changing the Way the Church Views Racism* (Harrisonburg, VA: Herald Press, 2016), 24.

78 Hart.

79 Caryll Houselander, *A Rocking-Horse Catholic* (New York: Sheed and Ward, 1955), 137–140.

80 Aquinas, *Summa Theologica*, I–II.26.4.

81 Cheryl C. D. Hughes, *Katharine Drexel: The Riches to Rags Story of an American Catholic Saint* (Grand Rapids, MI: William B. Eerdman's Publishing Company, 2014), 10.

82 Sherry Weddell, *Fruitful Discipleship: Living the Mission of Jesus in the Church and the World* (Huntington, IN: Our Sunday Visitor, 2017), 73.

83 Aquinas, *Summa Theologica*, I–II.111.a1.

84 Weddell, 103.

85 Weddell, 68.

86 Hughes, *Katharine Drexel*, 126.

87 Hughes, 124.

88 Hughes, 47.

89 Hughes, 161.

90 Hughes, 134.

91 Lisa Snowden-McCray, "The NAACP Was Established February 12, 1909," *The Crisis* (February 13, 2019), retrieved July 28, 2020.

92 Weddell, 78–79.

93 Archbishop Joseph Rummel to the clergy, religious, and laity of the Archdiocese of New Orleans, "Blessed Are the Peacemakers" (March 15, 1953), 5.

94 Helen Prejean, *River of Fire: My Spiritual Journey* (New York: Random House, 2019), 111–112.

95 Alfred C. Hughes, "Made in the Image and Likeness of God: A Pastoral Letter on Racial Harmony" (December 16, 2006), 15.

96 Braxton, "The Racial Divide in the United States," 9.

97 David W. Swanson, *Rediscipling the White Church: From Cheap Diversity to True Solidarity* (Downers Grove, IL: Intervarsity Press, 2020), 86.

98 Quote by St. Teresa of Calcutta found verified by the author at crossroadsinitiative.com/.

99 Available at usccb.org/. This prayer, first presented by Cardinal Dearden in 1979 and quoted by Pope Francis in 2015, is an excerpt from a homily written for Cardinal Dearden by then-Fr. Ken Untener on the occasion of the Mass for Deceased Priests, October 25, 1979. The words, often attributed to St. Oscar Romero (1917–1980), an El Salvadoran archbishop who was assassinated while celebrating Mass for preaching against the government's repression of human rights, were never spoken by him, but they speak to his spirit.

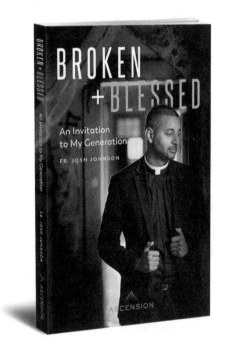

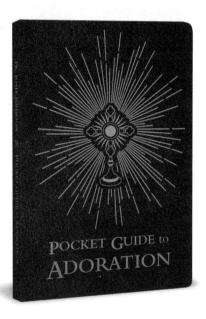

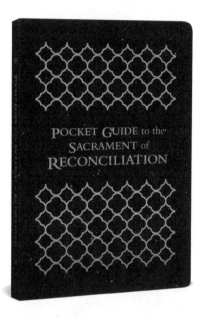